A CLOSE
HIS DARK

To our friends
Martyn and Sue
whose lives model the real thing

A Closer Look at
His Dark Materials

JOHN HOUGHTON

An Imprint of Cook Communications Ministries
COLORADO SPRINGS, COLORADO ● PARIS, ONTARIO
KINGSWAY COMMUNICATIONS, LTD., EASTBOURNE, ENGLAND

ISBN 1 84291 155 4

Victor is an imprint of
KINGSWAY COMMUNICATIONS LTD
Lottbridge Drove, Eastbourne BN23 6NT, England.
Email: books@kingsway.co.uk

Printed in the U.S.A.

Recent books by John Houghton include:

A Closer Look at Harry Potter
Fear Not (with Dave Roberts)
Making the Transition
Motivating for Mission
Oswain and the Battle for Alamore
Oswain and the Guild of the White Eagle
Oswain and the Mystery of the Star Stone
Oswain and the Quest for the Ice Maiden
Oswain and the Secret of the Lost Island
Out Here
The Covenants
The Letter to the Hebrews
The Letter to the Romans

Contents

Why the Fuss?

Following the publication of my book *A Closer Look at Harry Potter* I began to receive enquiries from readers, and especially concerned parents and teachers, asking me when I intended to tackle the Philip Pullman trilogy called *His Dark Materials* – *Northern Lights* (The Golden Compass, USA, 1995), *The Subtle Knife* (1997), *The Amber Spyglass* (2000). At that time I had not read this work but when I did so I realised that it merited a response.

Not that there are many similarities between the Harry Potter novels and *His Dark Materials*. The former follows a straightforward mythic structure similar to *Star Wars* and other popular tales, but Pullman's work is far more deeply textured, a cleverly woven tapestry dealing with profound philosophic, theological and psychological questions through the medium of a fascinating and inventive story. It is also polemical in its use of language; Pullman pulls no punches in his monochrome attack on the church and on God, showing little concern for the sensibilities of our postmodern ears, let alone the feelings of the devout.

Pullman, somewhat the darling of the intellectual establishment, to judge by the sycophancy of his interviewers and reviewers alike, describes himself unashamedly: 'I am of the Devil's party and I know it.'[1] How true that brash claim is requires an examination of his work and the issues that it raises. The *Daily Mail* headlined Philip Pullman: 'This is the most dangerous author in Britain' but to attack him with fundamentalist venom is to miss the point altogether and those who are expecting me to do that will be disappointed.

His Dark Materials – a line from John Milton's *Paradise Lost*, Book II – is a heady mix of science, theology and magic that proposes an alternative salvation for the human race and in so doing raises a number of matters vital for us to reflect upon as we wallow around in our postmodern sea of non-certainty. It also invites a fresh examination of the Christian faith and the extent to which it offers, if at all, a way forward in our search for meaning and belonging.

Some will immediately protest that *His Dark Materials* sets out to be no more than a story and a jolly good one at that. Why should we look any deeper? Why deconstruct the plot and spoil the artistry? Yet, quite apart from the fact that even a cursory reading shows that this is more than just an entertaining story, Pullman himself grants us tacit permission to do just that.

In the report of an interview given in August 2000 he states:

> But as I say, my aim is to tell a story which does have other resonances, if you like; some of them being moral. That's not to say I set out to preach. I'm in the wrong trade if I set out to preach. When you undertake a task of any length, of any sort of intellectual weight, when you set out to write a book that's going to take you seven years to finish, as I did with *His Dark Materials,* for example, then necessarily you do have some sort of moral commitment to it: you do it because you think it's a good thing to do. You wouldn't spend seven years doing something that you didn't believe in with some part of your moral being. So there is that dimension to it, yes. If that's what people want to see and talk about then that's fine; if they want to go for the story and ignore the other stuff equally that's fine. I'm not telling them

---

[1] *Observer*, 26 August 2001.

how to read any more than I'm telling them which people are allowed to and which aren't. I just tell the story that I want to tell.[2]

Furthermore, good fantasy as a medium can always be read at more than one level. Terry Pratchett's *Discworld* series contains many acute observations on human nature relevant to our own world, as well as being great fun to read. *The Lion, the Witch and the Wardrobe* by C. S. Lewis has delighted generations as a magical story but it can also be read as a metaphor for the death and resurrection of Christ. And what shall we say of the layers of meaning in the masterly *Lord of the Rings*, which itself is only a small segment of the multi-textured cosmic myth that J. R. R. Tolkien wove in *The Silmarillion*? *His Dark Materials* is no different and it would be doing the author an injustice not to look at its underlying values. A sermon it may not be, but a message it most certainly contains.

The aim of this book, then, is to concentrate only marginally on the literary merits of the work – which are considerable – and instead to focus on the subtext, examining those philosophic, theological and psychological values that invite our reflection and that challenge us, often forcibly, to re-examine our own beliefs. Since *His Dark Materials* is concerned with religion, and an attack on a perceived version of the Christian religion at that, I shall attempt to give what I think might be a biblical Christian response, though some of this will be no more than my own speculations. I am not a professional theologian, philosopher, molecular physicist, psychologist or literary critic, and the limitations and generalities of this work doubtless will be apparent to all. These are, after all, simply one man's reflections. However, I hope that this modest offering will at least have the virtue of accessibility and will unravel for some the complexities and ambiguities of the tale. In particular, I trust that those many friends of mine who are sincere

---

[2] This interview took place in August 2000, at Lexicon, a small literary convention (Unicon 2000) held in Oxford, England. An edited version of this interview (of which this is a lightly edited transcript) previously appeared in Locus#479, December 2000.

followers of Christ and who feel that their faith has been parodied and affronted will understand better two things: when Pullman is 'of the Devil's party' and arguing for a robust materialism over against otherworldliness; and when, in spite of himself, he gets perilously close to the truth and might be doing Christians a favour.

Rather than working chronologically through the story, I have chosen to group the major issues for reflection under my own chapter headings. This is partly to assist those who may not have read, or do not intend to read, *His Dark Materials* but who wish to know what it is about. It is also because the issues themselves are woven throughout the tale rather than coming up in any particular sequential order.

I am grateful for the help of a number of friends with whom I have aired the issues raised, and in particular to Keith Ives for his research on John Milton; to Richard Herkes for his notes on the trilogy; to Carol Hicks for faithfully transcribing my notes and typing the text; and to my wife, Jan, whose collaboration and encouragement always transforms a task into a pleasure.

Where references and quotations are appropriate I have used the paperback edition published in the UK by Scholastic Children's Books under their Point imprint, and I refer to the three volumes respectively in footnotes as *NL*, *TSK* and *TAS*, and to the entire trilogy as *HDM*. As far as possible I have tried fairly to separate Philip Pullman's personally expressed views on the matters raised by the story from those propounded within the story itself. Any error on my part is an error of oversight, not of intention. Other quotations are acknowledged as far as possible in the footnotes.

John Houghton
February 2004

1

A Matter of Life and Death

THE SOUL AND THE BODY, AND THE AFTERLIFE

His Dark Materials – Northern Lights, The Subtle Knife and *The Amber Spyglass* is a fascinating and somewhat controversial three-volume swashbuckling adventure involving parallel worlds and centring on the fortunes of a feisty young girl named Lyra, whose destiny it is to save the cosmos from catastrophe. At the same time it is a profoundly philosophic tale that raises many questions about the universe, religion and human consciousness. Those matters include: death and the survival of the soul; quantum theory and the nature of matter; the origins and plurality of universes; the nature of truth and deception; angels, witches and shamans; whether the Fall was upwards or downwards; political freedom and the abuse of power by religion; the origin and character of God; and the means of human salvation.

Moreover, at first sight it is a trilogy that reads as an overtly and militantly anti-Christian (and by implication anti-Jewish and anti-Islamic) polemic, with a target audience of older children and adolescents. The third volume won the Whitbread Prize for literature – the first children's book to do so.[1]

---

[1] Whitbread Book of the Year and Whitbread Children's Book of the Year 2001.

The first volume, *Northern Lights*, commences in the quasi-Victorian setting of an Oxford college called Jordan,[2] in which the author contrasts a stuffy brown academia with the sprightly antics of his heroine, Lyra Belacqua, and her daemon, Pantalaimon. The world is ours but not quite ours. Most of the science and technological invention is authentically Victorian and early Edwardian, but electricity, for example, is called anbaric force, probably from the Arabic *anbar*, meaning amber, synonymous with the Greek *electron*.[3] It's a writer's device to make an historically familiar world seem different. In fact the Victorian world did have electric trains running at Bush Mills in Northern Ireland as early as 1883 and electric street lighting was installed in Godalming in 1881. They had airships too, long before the world of Zeppelins. Anachronistically, Pullman's Victorians know how to use post-1940s atomic power but they describe chocolate by the ancient Aztec word 'chocolatl', while children eat cornflakes invented in 1906. This telescoping of history is a feature of *His Dark Materials*, notably when it comes to portraying the church in medieval Roman Catholic terms flavoured with later Presbyterian Calvinism.

Demon souls

With the evocative opening line 'Lyra and her daemon moved through the darkening hall', we are plunged at once into a world of mystery far removed from the scientific realism of modernity, and we discover that Lyra has a daemon. In fact so do all the humans, and the witches. Daemons are visible animal spirits that express the underlying emotions, character and instincts of the personality that more commonly in our world lie beneath the veneer of our personas. This is so in worlds other than Lyra's, including our own, though here the daemons are invisible to their possessors. In

---

[2] A name chosen perhaps because the River Jordan represents transition.

[3] Amber, or *electron*, becomes charged when rubbed. Hence, electricity.

his journey of self-discovery Lyra's friend, Will, living in a twentieth-century world, finds to his amazement that he too has a daemon.

At first sight, and maybe with contrived mischief, the term suggests that everyone has a demon in the classical religious sense of a familiar spirit; an alien malevolent creature bent on wreaking violence and tormenting the psycho-physical reality of the individual. After all, 'daemon' is just a transliteration of the Greek word *daimon* and Pullman provocatively insists at the start of the trilogy that the term should be pronounced demon. Yet it does have other meanings. Rudyard Kipling uses the term to describe the creative muse. He writes:

> Let us now consider the Personal Daemon of Aristotle and others, of whom it has been truthfully written, though not published:—
>
>> This is the doom of the Makers – their Daemon lives in their pen.
>> If he be absent or sleeping, they are even as other men.
>> But if he be utterly present, and they swerve not from his behest,
>> The word that he gives shall continue, whether in earnest or jest.
>
> My Daemon was with me in the Jungle Books, Kim, and both Puck books, and good care I took to walk delicately, lest he should withdraw ... When your Daemon is in charge, do not try to think consciously. Drift, wait, and obey.[4]

Earlier, Percy Bysshe Shelley used the term to describe a surreal force almost akin to spirit in *The Daemon of the World*:

>> The chariot of the Daemon of the World
>> Descends in silent power:
>> Its shape reposed within: slight as some cloud
>> That catches but the palest tinge of day
>> When evening yields to night.[5]

Although the idea of the muse may have influenced Pullman's choice of term, he is more obviously merely using the old

---

[4] Rudyard Kipling (1865–1936), *Something of Myself.*
[5] Percy Bysshe Shelley (1792–1822), *The Daemon of the World.*

Amerindian idea of the soul having the form and character of an animal spirit. Within those cultures, at times of heightened spiritual awareness, the animal daemon was said to become visible. So with Pullman, his daemons are not alien entities but are instead the equivalent of the human soul.

In *His Dark Materials* a child's animal or bird daemon is capable of rapid changes of form, but at puberty it settles down and becomes fixed for life. In our world this seems a rather depressing thought and while not exactly true to life, it is central to Pullman's plot. For this is a story about growing up and coming of age, and the dramatic changes that occur at puberty, particularly in Lyra and Will, are the fulcrum for the redemption of the cosmos. By settling the daemon's form and character the adult person is determined.

One's daemon is exceedingly precious – as a soul should be – and while it will guide and guard you, it also needs protecting. To lose it would be a tragedy beyond compare; to harm it would be a wilful crime. Indeed, so personal is one's daemon that it is taboo in Lyra's world ever to touch another person's daemon and to do so is akin to sexual abuse. When Lyra is caught snooping at Bolvanger – an experimental laboratory in Lapland – some men seize her, 'and suddenly all the strength went out of her. It was as if an alien hand had reached right inside where no hand had a right to be, and wrenched at something deep and precious. She felt faint, dizzy, sick, disgusted, limp with shock. One of the men was *holding* Pantalaimon. He had seized Lyra's daemon in his human hands ...'[6] It is difficult to avoid the implication of a sexual assault on a young girl in this harrowing account.

This tangled psychology of soul and sex is a recurring motif throughout the books, especially with the way that the church is supposed to sever children from their daemons – in other words, to tear out their souls. Much later, when Lyra and Will experience pubescent sexual intimacy, we find them stroking one another's

---

[6] *NL*, 276.

daemons, the taboo apparently abolished by adolescent love. There is also a manipulative sexual dalliance between Lyra's mother, Mrs Coulter, and one Sir Charles. When her monkey daemon seduces the man's serpent daemon, Pullman uses the unmistakable language of sexual foreplay.

The idea of animal daemons is nothing new, of course. Along with the Amerindians, people the world over have from time immemorial used animals to represent human traits. Even the modern world is replete with talking animals and birds – everything from the menagerie of the Narnia tales to the talking rabbits of *Watership Down* and the moles of *Duncton Wood*, to say nothing of the creatures in *Animal Farm, Wind in the Willows*, Brian Jacques' Redwall tales and my own Oswain tales. Then there's the old adage about people looking and behaving like their pet dogs and even an argument that says God put animals in the world precisely so that human beings would recognise their own behaviour from that of the creatures around them, and maybe learn a lesson or two. Proud as a peacock. Cunning as a fox. Timid as a mouse. Bold as a lion, and so on.

What is significant is that Pullman proposes that human beings, in all his worlds, do after all possess human souls. This will come as no news to those of a religious persuasion, or even to those who are the non-participating heirs of historic Christianity, but it comes as a surprise from an author who aligns himself with atheism and who has declared himself to be 'of the Devil's party'. This statement, incidentally, originates from a reflection by William Blake on the work of John Milton. Blake observed that Milton was of the devil's party and didn't know it.[7] Pullman says, 'I am of the Devil's party and I know it.'[8]

---

[7] 'The reason Milton wrote in fetters when he wrote of Angels & God, and at liberty when of Devils & Hell, is because he was a true Poet, and of the Devil's party without knowing it' (William Blake, *The Marriage of Heaven and Hell* [c. 1790–93]).

[8] *Observer* 26 August 2001.

To propose the existence of the human soul suggests that he may be less of the devil's party than he thinks. The age of modernity, with its crass materialistic obsession, sought progressively to deny that very thing. Psychology and sociology were profoundly influenced by the American psychologist B. F. Skinner (1904–90) and the behaviourist school that tried to argue that humans were just like animals; we were no more than stimulus–response mechanisms whose behaviour could be controlled by the reinforcements of reward and punishment to do whatever was demanded of us. A lot of inconclusive anatomical and psychological research was done to bolster the idea that the brain and the mind were synonymous and that all behaviour could be explained in terms of electrochemical stimulus and response. This cynical view of human nature, denying as it did the existence of an autonomous soul, was popularised by such books as *The Naked Ape* and *Manwatching* by Desmond Morris and this kept the notion going far longer than it warranted.

Meanwhile, Christianity and all the other great religions with a belief in the existence of the human soul found themselves relegated to the realms of whimsical fable. The denial of the soul obliterated the possibility of an afterlife and, to all intents and purposes, the existence of God. It is philosophically untenable to be a behaviourist and a theist. Yet the innate cry for human freedom that behaviourism so obviously denies did not go away. Arthur Koestler (1905–83) is an example of a non-Christian who did protest. He was a Hungarian writer who had seen the effects of behaviourist philosophy in the Stalinist purges. He understood first hand that it inevitably leads to dictatorial control by governments and the subverting of the psychiatric profession into the role of social conditioners rather than healers. His famous book, *The Ghost in the Machine*,[9] mounted a direct challenge to what he called 'nothing-but-ism'. Though by no means a Christian, Koestler argued cogently that humans were much more than the

---

[9] Hutchinson Publishing, 1967.

behaviourists would have them to be, and recent research into human near-death experiences suggests the possibility that mind might indeed exist outside the body.

Having spent years seeking to defend the existence of the soul as a distinct supra-physical component of human nature, maybe Christians should welcome Philip Pullman's notion of a daemon-soul after all. Indeed, he goes further: in his third book he has an apostate nun named Mary quoting the apostle Paul, where he talks about spirit and soul and body.[10] She says, 'The idea of three parts in human nature isn't so strange.' We may naturally wonder what an apostate nun is doing arguing for a tripartite human nature, but that is on a par with the ambivalence that is a characteristic of *His Dark Materials*. It comes about like this: Lyra is whizzing backwards and forwards between worlds and comes across an Oxford researcher named Dr Mary Malone. She is looking into Dark Matter – a notion we will consider later. Malone and Lyra strike up a friendship and much later Lyra and Will meet her in yet another world. Malone explains to them: 'I thought physics could be done to the glory of God till I saw there wasn't any God at all and that physics was more interesting anyway. The Christian religion is a very powerful and convincing mistake, that's all.'[11] She then proceeds to explain why she gave up being a nun. She had delivered a paper at a conference and gone to dinner with a nice man who reminded her of when she had been twelve years old and a boy had given her a piece of marzipan. Mary decided that she wanted love more than God, so she threw her crucifix into the sea. The Mary Malone who still wants to argue for a tripartite human nature is at the same time prey to the ludicrous suggestion that human love and God are mutually incompatible.

We find this same ambivalence in another scene, where Pullman distinguishes humans from animals precisely because animals do not have souls. There's an armoured bear named Iorek Byrnison,

---

[10] *TAS*, 463. See 1 Thessalonians 5:23.
[11] *TAS*, 464.

who can talk, work metal and drink alcohol, but he doesn't have a soul. He has a vain rival named Ioufur Raknison, who desires nothing more than to obtain a daemon, a human soul. Lyra, who befriends Iorek, uses this vanity as the lever to persuade Ioufur to engage in one-to-one combat with Iorek, rather than let his troops use a flame-thrower on him – a contest which Iorek wins.

At first sight this would seem quite consistent with a biblical creationist position. The book of Genesis declares Adam a distinct creation quite unlike the creation of the animal kingdom. Animals have life but man has a soul. God breathes the breath of life into the first man and he becomes a living being – literally *neshamah* producing *nephesh* (Genesis 2:7). Yet for Pullman human consciousness is not something God-given, as per Genesis, but is the result of an evolutionary process in which inanimate matter decided to become conscious. We must, however, leave this oxymoron until later and ask the more immediate question, 'What becomes of a daemon when a human dies?'

Beyond the grave

The answer in brief is that the daemon is absorbed into the ether and the spirit goes to the place of the dead – though Will and Lyra are destined to change all that. In the third volume they, along with creatures called Gallivespians, enter the world of the dead and meet some recently murdered people in their ghost form. They come to the town of the dead – a real dump of a place, a sort of ferry port where the dead wait to catch the boat. They are told that everyone is born with their death, and their death accompanies them through life until it taps them on the shoulder and says, 'Your time is up.' Lyra is told that the only way they can cross the sea to the place of the dead is to call up their own deaths.

This they do with passionate determination because Lyra wants to say goodbye to her dead friend Roger. The ferry boat comes for Will and Lyra, but to make the journey Lyra must leave her daemon, Pantalaimon, behind and it is heart-rending for her to do so. Will, who didn't know he had a daemon and had never seen it, leaves his behind too. Because they do this willingly, both Lyra and Will retain their spirits, so they are not actually dead. They reach the gates to the place of the dead, but before they can enter the gates they are attacked by Harpies. After battling through the gates, they find a vast dreary plain full of ghosts who are constantly tormented by the accusations of the Harpies.

Lyra and Will plan to release all the ghosts from the land of the dead and they form a treaty with the Harpies. When Will and Lyra have opened a way out, the Harpies will guide the ghosts through on the one condition that people tell them their true story. Since the daemons of the deceased are already one with nature, so the ghosts will leave the land of the dead to be rejoined with their daemons in a neat pantheistic unity.

Leaving aside the question as to whether this is good bedtime reading for impressionable children, it is in many respects a retelling of the old Greek mythological concept of Hades. Hades was one of the sons of Cronus, Lord of the Lower World, and came to represent the abode of the spirits of the dead. In Greek mythology Hades is as Pullman paints it: a grim place of endless despondency rather than a place of either evil or punishment. There is no garish Satan figure stoking the fires of a medieval hell, and it has little in common with the biblical use of the term.

Nevertheless, Pullman wants to say that this Hades is one of God's nastier inventions. There's a martyr in the story who comes forward and declares that she had been told she would go to heaven for her pains, but it was a lie: 'The land of the dead isn't a land of reward or a place of punishment. It's a place of nothing. The good come here as well as the wicked, and all of us languish in this gloom for ever.'[12] Then a mad monk accuses Lyra of deception and declares that this awful place of the dead is a blessed heaven compared to earth. It is paradise, no less!

---

[12] *TAS,* 336.

There is no heaven awaiting the faithful or the martyr or the loyal servant of the church. Paradise is a myth – presumably a lie told by the church to induce sacrificial devotion among its disciples, much like the lies told to suicide bombers – whereas in truth God cynically sends people to this squalid dump because of his vindictive nature. It is a calculated denial of Christian hope, but that hope has been perversely framed as the tragic Greek alternative, far removed from the biblical reality. Thus the scene is set for Lyra and Will to play the hero and set the ghosts free. Ignoring the mad monk and guided by the reformed Harpies, they lead millions of ghosts away from this land of shadows that was supposedly imposed by God.

Their heroic journey isn't altogether easy. In the place of the dead are the ghosts of a balloonist named Lee Scoresby, and Will's father, John Parry. They tell Will to cut the short hair from Lyra's head that was left when Mrs Coulter earlier had snipped off a lock. Will must put the short hair through the window of another world very quickly. He does so just in time: the church in a parallel world explodes a fearsome nuclear bomb containing the lock of Lyra's hair. The blast, targeted on Lyra, leaves them unscathed. However, the bomb opens a terrible abyss that adds to the difficulty of leading the ghosts to freedom.

In spite of all this, Lyra and Will succeed and the ghosts joyfully become one with the environment. In a scene reminiscent of the pop pantheism of the late 1960s, the hope of a true heaven is replaced by a pantheistic romanticised recycling unit: 'We'll be alive again in a thousand blades of grass, and a million leaves, we'll be falling in the raindrops and blowing in the fresh breeze, we'll be glittering in the dew under the stars and the moon out there in the physical world which is our true home and always was.'[13]

By the very nature of the subject, what, if anything, happens to us after death is a matter of some speculation. It's easy for those

---

[13] *TAS*, 336.

who believe that they are no more than sophisticated machines. They have no choice but to conclude that when the machine ceases to function, their consciousness dies, and that's all there is to it. However, those who believe in the existence of a soul, as the plot of *His Dark Materials* indicates, must decide what happens to that soul upon death.

The Greek view promised nothing but endless drabness for immortal disembodied beings, but can we find much more in the Old Testament concept of Sheol? When the prophet Isaiah writes, 'The grave [Sheol] enlarges its appetite and opens its mouth without limit; into it will descend their nobles and masses with all their brawlers and revellers' (Isaiah 5:14), it seems to offer less than the Greek view; just death, the grave, a realm of dust and darkness below the surface of the earth, a place of silence and forgetfulness, and to be avoided for as long as possible.

In the Hebrew mind life was for living. God was to be served, worshipped and enjoyed in the here and now. They were the people of God, and eternal life was corporate, experienced through the line of unbroken ancestry and future descendants. So strong was this thought that we might almost conclude that the Old Testament had no concept of the afterlife at all. Yet there is another side to the story and it is revealed in occasional illuminating flashes: 'Enoch walked with God; then he was no more, because God took him away' (Genesis 5:24); 'The Lord brings death and makes alive; he brings down to the grave and raises up' (1 Samuel 2:6); 'I know that my Redeemer lives, and that in the end he will stand upon the earth' (Job 19:25). Nor should we forget Elijah's dramatic and fiery departure (2 Kings 2:11–12) and that startling verse in the Psalms: 'God will redeem my life from the grave; he will surely take me to himself' (Psalm 49:15). Further, in Psalm 73 there's more than a hint of what was to become explicit in the New Testament: 'afterwards you will take me into glory' (Psalm 73:24).

Biblical realism faces the fact that death is the lot of the human race; it isn't something illusory. Yet nor is it natural. Death is a consequence of sin and rebellion against a God of love and is itself an enemy ultimately to be destroyed by Christ. The messianic Psalm 16, quoted in part by Peter on the day of Pentecost, holds the real key to understanding the afterlife, and it is surprisingly physical: '... my heart is glad and my tongue rejoices; my body also will live in hope, because you will not abandon me to the grave, nor will you let your Holy One see decay. You have made known to me the paths of life; you will fill me with joy in your presence' (Acts 2:25–28).

Peter was preaching about the resurrection of Christ and that is where the New Testament puts the emphasis. The soul is separated from the body at death, but it is certainly not a permanent state. The New Testament hope points to the return of Christ, when the body will be resurrected and reunited with the soul as sure as Jesus was raised from the dead himself. So Paul, in his grand chapter on the resurrection, can cry in triumph, 'Where, O death, is your victory? Where, O death, is your sting?' (1 Corinthians 15:55). Death will die and there awaits for the follower of Christ a renewed personal unity as a body-soul-spirit in a brilliant new heaven and new earth. Unlike the Greeks, with their notion of immortal souls trapped in an endless gloom, the New Testament writers anticipated a supra-physical life to come – and Jesus was the forerunner of what that will mean.

This isn't the place to rehearse the compelling proof for the resurrection of Christ, but we should note its implications. The fact that Christ was raised from the dead told the apostles that there was a spiritual world in which God was a living reality. It had been implied, of course. Jesus argued from the Old Testament scriptures that God being described as the God of Abraham, Isaac and Jacob was not a sequential truth but a simultaneous one (Luke 20:37–38). He was the God of all of them at once because he was not the God of the dead but of the living, indicating that these three great ancestors were all even now alive in the spirit. Jesus promised the dying thief who believed in him that even that very day he would be with Christ in paradise (Luke 23:43). And when he told the disciples that within his Father's house there were many mansions (John 14:1–3), the figurative language unmistakably indicates the reality of blessed experience in the presence of God.

But now the words had become action. Jesus didn't have a near-death experience; he really did die, and he really did rise again. Someone has come back from the grave and he is the most trustworthy man of all. Like they say on Easter Sunday, 'Christ is risen! Hallelujah!'

So the apostle Paul rightly understood that those who share in a spiritual union with Christ already participate in his resurrection life, and one day they will also participate in his physical resurrection. There's a time fixed for this and it's determined by the glorious return of Christ to this world when all those who have died in Christ will be physically raised from the dead and reunited with their souls. Those souls, however, have not been in limbo or purgatory, let alone a Greek Hades. They have spent the intermediate time in the joy-filled presence of God – a true paradise, no less. The apostle Paul lived his earthly life anticipating that one day he would be with the Lord; he saw his earthly body as a tent that would be destroyed, yet that was anything but the end of life. He would depart to be with Christ in a better state of existence (Philippians 1:23). There was a house waiting for him in heaven, not built by human hands but by divine (2 Corinthians 5:1–8).

This is a far cry from the suggestion in *His Dark Materials* that upon death people are immediately plunged into a drab, disembodied and permanent semi-existence because of the spite of a vindictive God. God doesn't wish that anyone should perish, whatever form that perishing might take (2 Peter 3:9). The whole point of the Christian gospel is that it invites people into loving fellowship with God, not the opposite. Of course, if people choose to reject that love, to continue a vain, egotistical lifestyle abusing others and disregarding God's laws of love, then in a cause and effect universe, they bear the consequences of their own actions.

That may be, of their own choice, to spend eternity in the utter absence of God's love or any kind of fellowship with others. Jesus, awesomely, called it outer darkness. The day of reckoning is, after all, quite reasonably the time when we are called to account for our choices (2 Corinthians 5:10). Don't blame God if you wilfully disregard the law of gravity and bang your head when you jump off a cliff. Hell was intended for the devil and his cohorts; humans should do their best to avoid it.

The gospel message is about the mercy of God towards sinful people, and because Christ bore the sin of the world, whoever sincerely wishes to be saved can be. Simple faith in Christ resulting in a changed character and lifestyle will allow anyone to face the prospect of judgement with a quiet confidence in the righteousness of Christ. If their names are in the Lamb's book of life, then the life by which they will be judged is the life of Christ himself. It's what Paul means when he says that believers' lives are hidden with Christ in God (Colossians 3:3).

Pullman's attempt at replacing heaven and hell with a pantheistic never-never land, thus depriving the Almighty of his sadistic glee in dumping the poor dupes in Hades in the first place, hardly bears comparison with the biblical promise of heaven in the presence of Christ and the anticipation of a revitalised cosmos. Though one might have thought that with his multitude of interconnected worlds Pullman could have allowed for that new heaven and new earth to be somewhere!

His Dark Materials paints the bleak Greek picture and then blames God for it, yet the reason so many Greeks became followers of Christ was precisely because the gospel set them free from their drab philosophy and gave them a genuine hope for the future. There may be figurative harps in heaven, but there are certainly no Harpies to contend with! People need no heroic Will and Lyra to drag their ghosts from hell so that they can be lost in the vagueness of an over-romanticised pantheistic world. The greatest hero of all has already opened the way for humans to receive back their full consciousness and integrity, and to dwell in a renewed universe saturated with the love of God. That brilliant writer, the apostle John, says:

> Now the dwelling of God is with men, and he will live with them. They will be his people, and God himself will be with them and be their God. He will wipe every tear from their eyes. There will be no more death or mourning or crying or pain, for the old order of things has passed away. He who was seated on the throne said, 'I am making everything new!' Then he said, 'Write this down, for these words are trustworthy and true.' (Revelation 21:3–5)

2

Dust to Dust

DUST, CASTRATION AND CONSCIOUSNESS

Philip Pullman is obsessed with dust and so is everyone else in *His Dark Materials*. But before we reach for the furniture polish we must hasten to add that this is no ordinary dust. It is dust with a capital D – from dust to Dust!

The meaning of Dust is revealed through the story: Pullman's heroine, Lyra, foils a plot by the master of the college to poison her uncle, Lord Asriel, an ambitious scientist and explorer who had recently returned from the far north where he was investigating the loss of an explorer named Grumman. During the course of his expedition, Lord Asriel succeeded in photographing Dust, a mysterious and normally undetectable substance that becomes detectable due to the ionising effects of the aurora borealis. He has also seen another world, a parallel universe in the sky, and is determined to reach it – and he has found the scalped head of Grumman, who appears to have fallen foul of the Bear King.

Later on at a party hosted by her mother, Mrs Coulter, Lyra discovers that Dust consists of non-interacting elementary particles that seem to be attracted to human beings, especially adults. Children, for a reason later to be revealed, don't attract Dust until adolescence.

The imperious Lord Asriel is later imprisoned by bears, but using his great personal power, he persuades them to build him a mighty mansion and scientific laboratory in the far north. This is so that he can fulfil his intention of breaching the boundary between the worlds. Lyra, with her friend Roger, manages to reach this mansion and after recounting her story to Lord Asriel – who turns out not to be her uncle but her father – she asks about Dust. He tells her that a Russian scientist – one Boris Rusakov[1] – discovered an elementary particle that was named Dust. Dust clusters around humans and their activity, but is not strongly attracted until children reach puberty. Lord Asriel is at first horrified to meet his daughter, but recovers when he sees Roger because he needs to sacrifice a child in order to blast a path into the other world.

Asriel succeeds in his attempt. Roger dies, and Lyra crosses the bridge into the new world by herself. There she meets up with another boy, whose name is Will. He has found his way into this other world from twentieth-century Oxford and he takes Lyra back into his Oxford, where she meets Dr Mary Malone, the lapsed nun. Malone is researching dark matter and explains that its existence is necessary to make gravity work because the visible universe doesn't make sense without the presence of some such material. The problem is, no one can detect it.

Dust, then, is Pullman's name for the dark material that the big bang theory finds necessary to make the physics of the universe work. This is a hypothetical material, required because, according to current mathematics, there just isn't enough visible and detectable matter to account for the way the universe behaves, particularly with regard to gravity. A crude analogy may help. Imagine a large set of bathroom scales holding a hundred people. We know the body mass of these people and the law of gravity tells us how much they should weigh. Yet the scales read much

---

[1] There does exist a physicist named Dr Boris Rusakov, who has lectured at Oxford in recent years, but whether this is a tribute to him is not known.

more. Then we notice spaces between these people, as though something were preventing them standing closer together. We may surmise that there are other invisible people also on the scales – dark matter, because we don't yet have a means of seeing them.

It is possible, of course, that the sums could be wrong, or even – heresy of heresies – the big bang theory could be wrong. Then again, there might actually be something out there that we cannot at present detect. Whatever may be the future discoveries of experimental physics, the notion of dark matter is a gift to someone who is reworking *Paradise Lost*, as Pullman claims, especially when John Milton so conveniently supplies the line:

> Unless the almighty maker them ordain
> His dark materials to create more worlds.[2]

Dark matter, Dust, cannot be detected by normal scientific instruments. However, in *His Dark Materials*, Lord Asriel has apparently found a way of recording the material as a halo of Dust surrounding adults and, to a much lesser extent, children. He can do this because in the northern regions of the world the fabric between the worlds is thinner, and Dust can be seen falling through the aurora borealis from another realm. As a scientific discovery it might be deemed worthy of further exploration and Asriel is bent on finding its source. Lord Asriel's images are reminiscent of Kirlian photography, which purports to show the aura around human beings, and maybe that's where Pullman got the idea.

Meanwhile, in twentieth-century Oxford, Dr Malone thinks she has found a particle that fits the bill for dark matter: a shadow particle or Shadow.

The world of Shadows

At this point we enter the realm of metaphysics. These Shadows turn out to be particles of consciousness. They are matter evolving

---

[2] *Paradise Lost*, Book II.

to consciousness, but can only be detected by a state of mind described by Keats as capable of being in uncertainties, mysteries, doubts, without any irritable reaching after fact and reason.[3]

These Shadows of Malone's prove capable of communication provided they are given a mechanism by which to do so, and she has invented just that – a computer called the Cave. The term and the Shadows are a tribute to Plato and his famous allegory of the cave where people lived in darkness but then came into the light by means of philosophy.[4]

Dust then is conscious, consciousness itself, and synonymous with Shadows – and it begins to talk to Malone through her computer. She is told that 30,000 years ago matter decided to become self-aware. I called this an oxymoron in the first chapter because it is hard to conceive that something not self-aware can make a decision requiring self-awareness to become self-aware. Some may find that a rather fatal flaw in the plot.

These Shadows, this Dust, as we noted, are particularly attracted to humans and their activities. Because children are fully human beings we might expect that Dust would fall equally on them and on adults. But it doesn't. Again we have the sexual connection; Dust is much more attracted to those who are sexually mature and, as in the case of Lyra and Will, when they engage in their first pubescent sexual act.

It's putting a lot onto puberty; children up to that point have personalities or souls that flit around and then suddenly they

---

[3] Keats (1795–1821) described the creative mind as 'Negative Capability' – the ability to be 'in uncertainties, mysteries, doubts, without any irritable reaching after fact and reason' (L 1:193, to George and Tom Keats, 27/12/1817).

[4] People untaught in the Theory of Forms are prisoners chained in a cave, facing the wall and unable to turn their heads. Behind them burns a fire, and its light is used by puppeteers to cast the shadows of real objects onto the wall. Unable to see anything else, the prisoners mistake the shadows for the real thing; the appearance for the reality. However, once people have been released by philosophy and have achieved reflective understanding, they can see the reality of the otherwise invisible Forms. They might then journey out of the cave into the full light, realising that even the names they gave to shadows are dependent upon the Forms themselves. For example, what we call a chair is dependent on the Form for its chair-ness, the true chair from which all chairs are derived (Plato, *The Republic*, 427–347 BC).

become fixed. They then attract Dust. It is a strange view of children and adolescence to suggest that consciousness, imagination, arrives only with sexual awareness. Arguably it is biological and psychological drivel; sexual maturation makes a considerable and obvious difference to children, but to connect it with the emergence of consciousness and experience seems quite nonsensical. Most children are perfectly self-aware long before they reach puberty, let alone before they engage in sexual activity. From a sociological perspective, given the problems that our society already has with underage sexual activity, we can only hope that the impressionable don't get the idea that they can grow up only by engaging in a premature sexual act.

There is another surprise waiting for us: late at night and using her Cave computer, dark matter tells Malone that there are uncountable billions of them and they call themselves angels. In fact, angels are creatures made of Dust. Spirit by nature. Matter by action. Conscious matter. And, given the sexual connection, perhaps salacious Dust; even salacious angels!

The idea of conscious matter was developed by Pierre Teilhard de Chardin, the evolutionary catholic who was popular during Pullman's youth. Teilhard de Chardin was a palaeontologist who wanted to unite evolution and Christianity. He understood evolution not simply as an explanation of the past, but as a guide to the future development of the human race in a biological space-time relationship with God. God, for Teilhard de Chardin, was not simply on high, transcendent, nor was he purely immanent or within. God was also ahead. In Teilhard de Chardin's understanding, this teleological aspect of evolution would take us to the omega point, when God is all in all.

Teilhard de Chardin described this as a superior form of pantheism, 'the expectation of perfect unity, steeped in which each element will reach its consummation at the same time as the universe'.[5] He formulated a law to explain how the discernible

---

[5] Pierre Teilhard de Chardin (1881–1955), *Hymn of the Universe*.

direction of the universe worked. He called it the Law of
Complexity Consciousness, or Teilhard's Law: as matter evolves
towards complexity, so there is a corresponding rise in the
consciousness of matter. Using a rather crude analogy of spheres,
he coined the term 'noosphere', or mind-sphere, to describe this,
the next level of evolution.

Pullman has used Teilhard de Chardin's evolutionary notion of
conscious matter but has most certainly discarded his Catholicism.
Indeed, he does little to hide his hatred of it. In Lyra's world the
church is a parodied medieval Roman Catholic organisation
exercising immense and tyrannical power – and just to include the
Protestants, its last pope was John Calvin and it now has its power
base in Geneva, rather than Rome. For reasons never made clear,
the Magisterium in Geneva has decided that Dust is the physical
evidence for original sin. (We shall discover later that original sin
is not what we thought it was.) This far-fetched and unsubstanti-
ated connection leads the church to fear Dust, to hate it and to
seek ways of preventing it falling on humans, believing that if it
could do so, it could curb the effects of original sin.

This is where the plot gets labyrinthine, not to say contradictory.
Mary Malone's talking Shadows tell her that the first manifestation
of this newly conscious Dust was the first angel and this first angel
decided to boss all the other angels around and called himself God.
In fact, he took to himself all the names of the Old Testament God.
So Dust is particles of consciousness and these coalesced are
angels, and the first is called God. Yet the church, believing
naturally in angels and in God, is trying to destroy Dust, which is
angels and God. But since God is a pseudo-God, arguably the
church could be doing the right thing. Yet clearly it isn't because
Dust is good – unless it calls itself God, or sides with him, and
then it is bad!

Leaving aside for the moment the rather offensive anti-Semitic
suggestion that the God of the Jews is a liar, we need to ask why
this first lot of Dust, this first angel, should tell a lie. Where does
the lie come from? Is the lie evil? If it is not, then we have no

reason to oppose this first angel, whatever he calls himself. If it is evil, then we're still left with the problem of the origin of evil.

The problem is compounded when a whole bunch of Dust-constituted angels decide to rebel against the tyranny of the first angel. It leads to a heavenly punch-up which the first angel wins, and from then on he calls himself the Authority. So we're left now with good Dust and bad Dust; good angels and bad angels. Which ones shall we trust? How do we know that it's the good Dust that is speaking to Mary Malone? And if the rebel angels (i.e. good Dust, which is called by the church bad Dust) settle on human beings, why should not the bad Dust (the non-rebel angels, presumably loved by the church) also settle on human beings? Tenuously, the Shadows, who call themselves rebel angels (i.e. good angels), tell Malone that they intervened in human evolution to cause the original sin of consciousness out of vengeance for their defeat by the Authority. However, it didn't work properly and now consciousness is fading from the universe. Good consciousness *and* bad consciousness? We are meant to understand that it is only the rebel Dust that is fading. Whatever, Mary Malone is instructed to play the part of the serpent when she finds Will and Lyra, and to effect a second Fall so that it can come right next time round.

Lyra herself, with a child's logic, having learned of the existence of Dust and having seen the appalling behaviour of her mother and father and the church, concludes that if they treat Dust as evil, then it must in reality be good, so she decides to help Dust. Unfortunately the situation is worsening. Lord Asriel's violent wrenching of the fabric between the worlds, and the church's desperate attempt to destroy Lyra by means of a quantum bomb, has resulted in Dust flowing out of the universe faster than it can be made. If things carry on, there will be no consciousness left and everybody will be reduced to a zombie-like existence.

All this Mary Malone figures out while living with some odd, wheeled creatures called Mulefa – a reworked idea from a fantasy called *Ozma of Oz* by L. Frank Baum (1907). Mulefa are a kind of hybrid elephant on wheels that can see Dust and that live in a symbiotic relationship with it and in harmony with their environment. With their help, Mary invents an instrument, the Amber Spyglass, that allows her to see what is going on, and it inspires her to prevent this loss of consciousness. She does so by persuading Will and Lyra to sin – though as we shall see later, this is a 'good' sin.

Dust is for Pullman a sort of universal consciousness permeating the universe, existing before and after us. In an article in *Readerville Forum* he suggests that Dust enriches us and is nurtured in turn by us in a mutually beneficial relationship. There are shades of the Force in *Star Wars* here, but Pullman sees it less in Taoist terms and more as a simplistic form of pantheism. He says, 'Instead of being the dependent children of an all-powerful king, we are partners and equals with Dust in the great project of keeping the universe alive. It's a republican relationship, if you like, not a monarchical one. I don't find it difficult to think that Dust might suggest a new kind of relationship with a God.'[6]

Soul severance

The church, as we have noted, is supposed, outlandishly, to have concluded that Dust is the physical evidence of original sin. As it happens, it turns out that the church is correct, except for the fact that in *His Dark Materials* original sin is a good thing. The church, having noted that Dust falls more on adults than on children, begins to research ways of preventing Dust falling on children. Exercising its power through various societies, it allows

---

[6] 'Dust permeates everything in the universe, and existed before we individuals did and will continue after us. Dust enriches us and is nurtured in turn by us; it brings wisdom and it is kept alive by love and curiosity and diligent enquiry and kindness and patience and hope. The relationship we have with Dust is mutually beneficial. Instead of being the dependent children of an all-powerful king, we are partners and equals with Dust in the great project of keeping the universe alive. It's a republican relationship, if you like, not a monarchical one. I don't find it difficult to think that Dust might suggest a new kind of relationship with a God' (*Readerville Forum*).

Mrs Coulter, Lyra's mother, to set up the General Oblation Board. Its agents become known as the Gobblers because they abduct children, including Lyra's original playmate Roger, the kitchen boy at Jordan College, and a child from the canal boat people – known as gyptians – along with many others. The term 'oblation' comes from the medieval notion that children could be given to the church as an offering to be trained as monks or nuns, and the task of this Board is to offer children to God unsullied by original sin; that is, by Dust.

We might note in passing that since Dust is supposed to be angels, one would expect that it would fall more easily on children than upon adults, particularly in the light of Jesus' words about the close relationship between angels and children (Matthew 18:10). But many things are reversed in 'the Devil's party', and in *His Dark Materials* the church decides that the best way to cancel the effects of original sin is to prevent the personality fixing by cutting off the daemons altogether – effectively castrating growing up. Since this equates to tearing out the soul, the church, which historically has more to say about the soul than anybody else, is now supposed to want to get rid of souls!

Lyra discovers all this when she and the gyptians decide to go north to rescue the children. They raise money and hire a ship which takes them to the Norwegian peninsula. Surviving an attack by a lethal mechanical fly operated by a daemon, and capturing it in a tin on the way, they arrive at Trollshund in Lapland. There they hire the services of Iorek Byrnison, an armoured bear who is presently banished from his pack and now serves as a mechanic, divested of his armour in punishment for killing humans. Lyra enables the bear to get his armour back, which he does with great violence. Being loyal to his word, he agrees to accompany the gyptians on a sledge trip into the northern darkness. At one point, riding on Iorek's back, Lyra reaches a village to find the horror of a poor abandoned lad whose daemon has been removed from him, reducing him almost to an animal state. Out of compassion, Lyra takes the boy back to the gyptians, but he dies overnight. However, they now know that the Gobblers cut off the soul, or the daemon, from children.

The process is called intercision – perhaps a play on the word 'intercession' and a cheap jibe at the church. It's described in pretty horrendous detail and calculated to make all of us hate any organisation that could do such an evil thing as to destroy the souls of children. But that is how the church is presented in *His Dark Materials*; indeed, we are told explicitly that the church mutilates children. In fact, that all churches mutilate children.[7] It's not exactly a subtle way of warning children off churches in our present world!

This emotive connection between castration and intercision and the desire to cure original sin by cutting off consciousness almost equates consciousness with sexual desire. If so, it would give us a very limited perception of consciousness. Surely Pullman isn't proposing a pantheistic fertility cult as the maturation of human progress? The association of castration with curing original sin is also reminiscent of the 1960s nonsense that suggested the church was anti-sex and anti-sexual pleasure, which it manifestly isn't. And it is, of course, a ludicrous idea to suggest that original sin has anything to do with sex. Even an elementary reading of the Genesis account demonstrates that it doesn't. Adam and Eve were instructed to enjoy sexual pleasure and to have children before ever Eve fell for the serpent's temptation (Genesis 1:28; 2:22–25).

It might be said, of course, that the whole of *His Dark Materials* is a realm of parody in which many things are consciously warped. There is an element of truth in this and it may serve a good purpose in the way that a distorting mirror may nonetheless help us to see at least something about our true shape, or at least make us determined never to look like that particular reflection. Yet 'the Devil's party' is ever subtle, relying on insinuation, half truth and

---

[7] '– they cut their sexual organs, yes, both boys and girls – they cut them with knives so that they shan't feel. That is what the church does, and every church is the same: control, destroy, obliterate every good feeling' (*TSK*, 52).

suggestion, and in an age of widespread ignorance regarding the Christian faith we must assume that some at least will take the parody for the truth. We owe it to them to set the record straight, if only so that they can, from a literary perspective, better appreciate the cleverness of Pullman's twists and turns.[8]

Lyra is destined to find out firsthand what intercision means. The gyptians are travelling to a place called Bolvanger in almost perpetual darkness, when suddenly they are attacked by Tartar soldiers and Lyra is taken captive. She finds her old friend Roger, along with the other children, being prepared for intercision. Resourcefully, she creates a diversion during a fire practice, and Lyra and Roger discover that the daemons are kept in glass jars in a special room. With the aid of a friendly witch's daemon, they set them free. Just as Lyra is planning an escape, an airship arrives bearing none other than Mrs Coulter, her evil mother. Lyra manages to overhear a conversation between the scientists and Mrs Coulter, and she discovers that they have invented an alloy blade of manganese and titanium that can separate a daemon from a child by putting the child and the daemon into separate cages and then slicing the blade down like a guillotine.

After Mrs Coulter leaves the room, the scientists discover Lyra and take her for immediate intercision. Just in time, Mrs Coulter rescues her daughter. Thoroughly terrified, Lyra plays along with her mother and is taken to a room where Mrs Coulter's own daemon, a sadistic monkey, accidentally lets loose the deadly fly

---

[8] Male castration has been performed since time immemorial, either as a punishment or as a means of producing trustworthy harem guards. In later times the Italian aristocracy practised castration on young boys during the seventeenth and eighteenth centuries, they being in great demand for the Italian opera. It was not something the church authorised, though being the great patron of the arts that it is, the Roman Catholic church did allow castrati to sing in the Vatican chapel as late as the nineteenth century before the practice was outlawed. Female castration is still practised in many sub-Saharan nations among the tribal peoples, but they are pretty consistently peoples that lack either Christian or Islamic orthodoxy because both of these faiths have always been totally opposed to the practice. In modern times, Hitler's Germany used castration and sterilisation as a political weapon to deal with undesirables. To identify the church with the practice of castration is frankly dishonest.

from its tin. This attacks Mrs Coulter, allowing Lyra to start a fire and lead the other children to escape.

Lord Asriel is a scientific imperialist prepared to make any sacrifice in the interest of progress. Aided by a balloonist named Lee Scoresby, some friendly witches on broomsticks and the new king of the bears, Iorek Byrnison, Lyra and Roger escape from Bolvanger and find their way to Lord Asriel's laboratory in the north. Lord Asriel explains to Lyra that Mrs Coulter is power hungry, first trying to get power through marriage and then through the church. So she set up this agency, the General Oblation Board, specialising in Dust research. The severance of daemons was permitted by the church, and because Mrs Coulter did it far away in the north everybody could turn a blind eye. She, of course, was only working on a theory that the change in one's daemon at adolescence and the fact that Dust begins to settle may be connected. In fact, all she could do was create zombies, which is presumably why she rescued Lyra.

Lord Asriel is aware that when the severance was made, a fractional but immensely powerful energy was released, which might be harnessed. Lyra goes to bed and is woken by Asriel's servant to say that he has left, taking Roger with him, because he needs a child to finish his experiment. Lyra realises with horror what she has done. Asriel wanted a child and she has brought him Roger. She sets out at once with Iorek to chase after Asriel, but they are attacked on the way by Mrs Coulter and a clan of witches. Iorek's bears use a flame-thrower to bring down the Zeppelin and, leaving the bears to fight it out, he and Lyra press on until they reach a chasm with a bridge of ice that could carry a child, but not an armoured bear. So Lyra crosses the bridge just before it collapses and, too late, she finds Lord Asriel and Roger. Asriel's daemon, a snow leopard, has captured Roger's daemon and Asriel is making connections with his apparatus and drawing power down from the aurora borealis by means of an aerial held up by a witch. In a final tussle, Roger's daemon is torn away and as Lyra and he teeter on the brink of an avalanche the aurora opens to reveal a dry, sunlit land in the sky. But Roger is dead.

Although we might have little patience with Pullman's indicting of the church, nonetheless, in the power-hungry attitudes of Asriel and Coulter, we do see a hint of where the blame for such barbarism should lie, and that is with the state and with a scientific imperialism that arrogantly believes we can take control of our own evolutionary destiny and recreate man in our own image, selecting those who will live and those who will not. For whatever the few castrati that the church indulged in time past – and it was wrong ever to do so – it hardly compares to the 6.6 million souls which, in Britain alone over the past thirty years, have been severed from their consciousness by its secular humanist establishment. It is a story of the most terrible and absolute form of intercision, practised not by the church, but by the state as a means of social control. Indeed, it is consistently opposed by Christians because it constitutes the most barbaric severance of a child.

At the risk of digression, but to make the point forcibly, here is one absolutely true story. Only the name has been changed.

Mary Smith became pregnant when she was sixteen, though she had been sexually active for a good while longer. Pressed by her state-employed doctor and the state-employed social worker, she agreed to have the child aborted. The hospital was efficient and polite. 'This is the right thing to do, Mary. It's all for the good,' she was told. Already she could feel the quickening of the young life within her womb. 'But it's only a piece of foetal matter. It can feel nothing. It has no consciousness,' they lied to her. Mary was instructed to remove her clothes and to don a hospital gown. Feeling neither ill nor in pain, she waited her turn in the impersonal glass and plastic hospital waiting room with its cold striplights and sanitised stainless steel machinery.

Perhaps it was the sound of other mothers with their babies. Maybe it was the nursery pictures on the wall. Whatever, all at once Mary realised that she was making a terrible mistake. Anxiety welled in her chest; she found it difficult to breathe. This was her baby and they wanted to take it away. Mary was no fool. Her baby would be inconvenient to the state. It dawned on her with blinding clarity that all it needed was time for that embryonic consciousness to develop and her baby would be a living, communicating person just like herself. And she was more than an incubator. She was a mother to be – no, already a mother.

Then the junior houseman came. 'All right?' he smiled brightly. 'Just a little premed to make you relax.'

'No, I don't want to go through with this.' Mary blurted the words out.

The houseman was bemused and called the senior physician. Together they tried persuasion, but Mary had made up her mind. Then the unthinkable happened. The doctor plunged the premed into her arm and instructed that she be taken down to the operating theatre at once. Mary struggled, screamed and fought on that whole journey, until they were actually holding her down on the operating table and the anaesthesia took over. Against her will, the doctor inserted a suction pump into the most private recess of her body and pressed the switch. In seconds the living baby, that human consciousness, that soul, was torn from her body to disappear down the tube as just so much refuse.

When Mary returned to consciousness, she awoke as a hollow woman, empty, devoid of life.

That disgusting intercision was practised on her not by a malevolent church, but by a callous and arrogant humanistic state. It's not the church that mutilates children. Far from it. No one does more to respect and defend the souls of the innocent and the vulnerable than Christians. It's the humanistic world that advocates the destruction of children's lives before they ever have a chance to enjoy consciousness.

The children severed from their daemons in *His Dark Materials* become zombies. This is another area where the modern secular state has been culpable – this time in the realm of psychiatry. Millions of people were zombified in the twentieth century by means of lobotomisation. Hitler and Stalin did it, and even in the

United States by 1959 the number of state-sanctioned lobotomised people exceeded 100,000. Lobotomisation was the loathsome practice of driving little chisels under the eyelids and into the brain to separate the frontal lobes of the brain from the rest in an attempt to control schizophrenia, or at least those whom the state judged to be schizophrenic. I suggest that this horrible mistake wasn't Christianity. It was secular humanism.

In appraising *His Dark Materials* we have a legitimate concern about its impact on the children targeted by the publishers. Many children nurture a faith of their own; they have a simple but genuine trust in God. Many are reared within the context of good churches. Is it right, even by implication and in a parallel world, to attack the beliefs of such children by telling them that the church is evil and that their faith is dangerous to their very health and identity? We need not advocate barmy political correctness, but respect for the faith of others is the least that we in this postmodern generation have come to take as a mark of civilised maturity. Is Pullman not in danger of practising his own form of intercision on children when he writes as he does? This is not a call for censorship. Atheists have as much right to write and publish their stuff as Christians, but the ethical question remains, and parents and teachers alike should be aware of it.

God in the distance

Returning to the matter of Dust and pantheism, we need to ask why Teilhard de Chardin should propose the idea of God being some kind of universal mind, and why that became so popular in the 1960s. Society was changing rapidly. The post-war generation had come of age and no longer felt at home with the rigid militarism of older generations. That generation had perceived God in overly transcendent terms; indeed, often to the point of Deism – a God so removed from us that he was effectively unknowable. God was immortal, invisible, only wise, but we wanted intimacy. He was a heavenly autocrat more akin to the deterministic Allah of

Islam than the God of the Bible, but we offspring of understandably emotionally repressed parents wanted to discuss our feelings. In 1963 Bishop John Robinson tried to address the issues with his book *Honest to God*, but rather than pointing us to the incarnation of Christ and the presence of the Holy Spirit to straighten out our perceptions of God the Father, he attempted to present God, in Paul Tillich's phrase, as 'the ground of our being'. It was a reaction: Robinson was trying to direct us to the personal immanent nature of God within us because he could no longer relate traditional faith concepts to the modern world.

The attempt by Teilhard de Chardin, Robinson and others did not succeed. Millions left the liberal church for the plain reason that if God was within you, then you hardly needed to go to church to be a Christian. If fact all you had to do was be generally decent. It was then only a step further to argue that God was your own inner consciousness, and that could be nurtured by techniques imported from the mystic East. The New Age movement and flower power was born. Inspired by rock, fuelled by pot and pleasured by free love (casual sex), we entered the Age of Aquarius, a gentle pantheistic paganism where all was oneness, peace and harmony. Thus transcendental consciousness replaced the old God consciousness, and the age of Christendom was over. At least, so it seemed at the time.

Of course, it hasn't worked out like that. The world is anything but peace and harmony. All that Jesus prophesied about 'wars and rumours of wars' (Matthew 24:6) continues because human nature remains the same. Meanwhile, working for peace the world over, a revitalised and renewed Christian faith is flourishing as never before. Maybe that's why Pullman feels the need to recycle these old 1960s notions through the medium of *His Dark Materials*.

A biblical approach to the nature of God, as opposed to a sociological one, sees him as simultaneously God most high and God most nigh; he is both distinct from his creation and at the same time intimately involved with it. Nowhere is this latter aspect more clear than in the incarnation of Christ where 'the Word became flesh and made his dwelling among us ...full of grace and truth' (John 1:14). But this is more than an historical phenomenon; in a telling phrase the apostle Paul describes the ascended Christ as the one that 'fills everything in every way' (Ephesians 1:23). It implies an intimacy with creation that may suggest that if dark matter exists it could prove to be no less than the consciousness of Christ himself. To use Stephen Hawking's pregnant phrase: the fire in the equations.[9]

The ascended Christ, being the Son of God, is distinct enough from creation (i.e. he is not material of the made kind) to avoid all the difficulties with pantheism, but close enough for us to say there is a known and loved person whose presence infuses and energises the entire created universe.[10]

Once again Pullman is reaching in the right direction and may prove to be less on the devil's side than he thinks. At least he is challenging a merely materialistic understanding of the universe – though he is still trapped by materialism because his idea of consciousness is not truly transcendent but merely a developed variety of the material. It's still a journey to the cosmic Christ.

The problem of cosmic alienation is nothing new. We can go back to 1000 BC and find Solomon the Wise, who, having tasted the delights of materialism and despairing of the human condition, faced the same yearning: 'He has made everything beautiful in its time. He has also set eternity in the hearts of men; yet they cannot fathom what God has done from beginning to end' (Ecclesiastes 3:11). Then there's Zophar the Naamathite taunting poor suffering Job with the question, 'Can you fathom the mysteries of God?' (Job 11:7). These things have vexed people for a long time. But

---

[9] 'What is it that breathes fire into the equations and makes a universe for them to describe?' (Stephen Hawking, *A Brief History of Time*, 1988).

[10] This idea risks falling foul of the 'God of the gaps' problem: if we don't know the answers then we call it God, which is fine until scientists find the answers and as they do so God progressively shrinks from the scene. There might be another explanation for dark matter, should it prove to exist. But Christ will still fill everything in every way; we will just need a better explanation of what that phrase means.

God is still closer than people think. When Paul addressed the pagans on Mars Hill in Athens he presented them with the astonishing news that God 'is not far from each one of us. For in him we live and move and have our being' (Acts 17:27–28). For all his transcendence, God isn't distant and unknowable. Jesus Christ is God made truly accessible. The apostle John says, 'No-one has ever seen God, but God the One and Only, who is at the Father's side, has made him known' (John 1:18).

If the Christ non-materially fills every molecule of the universe, then we are surrounded and infused by his personality wherever we go. The material world is constantly sanctified by his presence; the whole earth is filled with his glory. We no longer search for God like a needle in a haystack, nor despair at his unknowability, because his presence is there, around us and within us, and the whole universe pulsates with his life and consciousness.[11]

There remains the question, 'How do we make contact with this cosmic Christ or cosmic consciousness?' By prayer, or by technology. Lyra and Mary Malone both use occult divination, Lyra with an ancient instrument called an alethiometer and Malone with a modified hi-tech computer and I-Ching sticks. The problem with the technological approach is that it inevitably leads to Gnostic elitism and to the formation of a specialised priesthood. Pullman, in his parody of the church, charges it with having a power-hungry priesthood, yet he is obliged to have shamans like Will's father, John, and occult adepts like Lyra and Mary, who are themselves acting as priests, and at the end of the trilogy Lyra is sent to an Oxford Dame who will teach her degree-level divination to enable all the lesser mortals to know what is going on. It hardly fosters spiritual democracy. Whereas in the New Testament God offers an interactive relationship with himself available to any and

---

[11] This gives us an insight into the mystery of suffering. Christ inhabits both the molecules of joy and the molecules of pain. He celebrates along with us but he also empathises with our sufferings, and he does so redemptively. The joy anticipates the greater delight of a renewed cosmos; the pain reminds us that the leaves of the tree are being used for the healing of the nations (Revelation 22:2).

everyone who comes to Christ in the simplicity of prayer. It needs no special preparation. No great learning. No sophisticated pride-serving techniques. Just the wisdom of children who know how to ask.

3

How Many Verses?

His Dark Materials might have been written as a comedy in the manner of a French farce what with all these people whizzing between worlds and popping up with almost comic predictability. Except that there is no comedy; this is a sombre story markedly short on humour (a weakness acknowledged by the author) – a tragedy no less. For this is a cosmos on the brink of war and the stakes are high; God must be destroyed and the church thwarted if the universe is to retain its consciousness and build a new future. And the story will end with two adolescent friends who can never meet again.

The cosmic nature of the tragedy is revealed by the interconnectivity of the many worlds. What happens in one has implications for all the others. When Lyra reaches Lord Asriel in his northern laboratory, he takes her into a measure of confidence and explains that Dust is coming into their world from another universe that can be seen through the aurora borealis, and that it is but one of millions of parallel worlds. These have been known about by witches for centuries, and by some theologians who have, predictably, been excommunicated by the church.

Worlds and windows

Lord Asriel is evidently ahead of his time and has a fair
understanding of quantum physics and the big bang theory.
According to the theory, at the very beginning of the universe all
the possibilities that could ever be were present, but at the moment
one possibility became an actuality all the other possibilities
ceased and the elementary particle form of our universe was
decided. This is more philosophy than physics – metaphysics
rather than mathematics – in our current stage of research.
However, a spin-off from the theory is to speculate that all those
unused other possibilities could bring parallel universes into
existence and there might be some connection between them.
Readers of children's comics like *The Beano* will recall that when
the artist wants to portray an explosion he draws something that
represents a big blast, like a puff of steam from a kettle, but it
often has little blasts coming off from the main stream as well. In
the big bang theory it's possible that these little blasts could have
formed into their own universes in the first fractions of a
millisecond after the bang. If other universes did come into being,
could we know about them, and could we travel to them? More
daringly, could what happens in one of the multi-verses affect
things in the others? Pullman boldly answers, yes.

When the mad church sets off its bomb to destroy Lyra, it does
so in a different world from the one she is then inhabiting.
Interestingly, the connection is a lock of her hair, stolen by her
mother but used without her consent, and placed within the bomb.
Will, as we noted, has to cut off the remaining hair and thrust it
into a third world to divert the force of the blast from Lyra. Here
we touch upon particle physics and the notion of quantum
entanglement – the idea that related objects will be affected by one
another wherever they are in the universe. At the subatomic level
of the quark (hypothetical elementary particle), a positive spin on,
say, one quark will affect its partner wherever that partner is in the
universe. Pullman has amplified this concept to the macro-level.

Indeed, the fate of Dust itself is dependent upon what happens between the worlds. If it is seeping out of one world, then it is seeping out of all the worlds into the abyss, and the act of 'sin' that Lyra and Will must perform will prevent Dust from being lost in all the universes.

Earlier, when Lord Asriel builds his bridge from Lyra's world into the one he can see through the aurora borealis, it upsets everything throughout the entire multi-verse. It is a piece of scientific imperialism and arrogance and pure melodrama. Asriel quite callously destroys Roger in order to achieve his goal, and the next minute Mrs Coulter turns up with her golden monkey. Before we know it she's clasped in Lord Asriel's arms, standing on the brink of the worlds, both of them intoxicated by their arcane sense of power, believing that it will be the end of the church, of the Magisterium, of the darkness – because the church will not be able to prevent people from crossing to another world, Lord Asriel says. So Asriel invites Mrs Coulter to join him in the new world to find the source of Dust and to stifle it for ever.[1]

Quite apart from the modern spin of involving quantum physics, journeying between worlds is nothing new, of course. We may cite Lewis Caroll's *Alice in Wonderland* and C. S. Lewis's Narnia tales to name but two examples. Somewhat pettily, Pullman has expressed a profound antipathy towards the latter for reasons that do not seem satisfactory, but it doesn't stop him using the same idea of journeying between worlds.[2]

Theoretical physics suggests that wormholes, based upon the curvature of time and space, may provide a shortcut between

---

[1] *NL*, 394. In the event, and somewhat puzzlingly, Mrs Coulter decides to remain behind. Later on in the third book, when Asriel and Mrs Coulter meet up again, it turns out that he was actually trying to save Dust, and by then she was intent on saving Lyra. It almost seems as if the author changed his plot halfway through and it hasn't worked too well.

[2] 'C S Lewis comes from a different tradition: in the Narnia books he struggles with big ideas. I dislike the conclusions he comes to because he seems to recommend the worship of a God who is a fascist and a bully; who dislikes people of different colours and who thinks of women as being less valuable in every way' (*The Guardian*, 2 March 2001).

worlds. More prosaically and perhaps obviously inspired by Mr Bill Gates and the Microsoft Corporation – 'Where do you want to go today?' – Pullman uses windows. However, he has something more sophisticated than a mouse or a keyboard. It's called the subtle knife, or Aesahaettr, meaning 'God-destroyer'. This is a double-sided knife: one blade is infinitely sharp and can cut through anything, and the other can tease open windows between the parallel worlds. It might serve as a very effective metaphor for the writer's pen.

In the second volume, Will Parry takes his demented mother to be looked after by his former piano teacher and returns to his own house to find government agents breaking in, looking for his missing father's papers. After accidentally killing one of the men, he flees to Oxford, and on the northern outskirts sees a cat walk through an invisible window into another world. He follows and it takes him to a deserted seaside town, where he encounters Lyra. It's not long before another boy and girl turn up – locals who tell them that they are in the city of Cittagazze and that some creatures called Spectres have frightened all the grown-ups away. The children can't see Spectres and they are unaffected by them, but if a Spectre catches a grown-up it eats the life out of them until they are hollow on the inside. Later on, Will works out that his mother was not entirely mad, but herself was being persecuted by Spectres in twentieth-century Oxfordshire. These Spectres will later prove to be the reason for the tragic end of the entire story.

Cittagazze, the City of Magpies (because of their thievery of bright things), is the central world, the hub for the multitude of interconnecting windows that unites this cosmological honeycomb. It is reminiscent of the pools of water in the wood between the worlds that C. S. Lewis uses in *The Magician's Nephew*.

A flock of witches led by one Serafina Pekkala have come by their own window into Cittagazze looking for Lyra, when they observe an attack of the Spectres of Indifference, as they are known, on a group of travellers. The adults quickly turn into zombies, but the children are unharmed. From two adult survivors, they discover that the philosophers of the Guild of the Torre degli Angeli, the Tower of Angels in Cittagazze, found a way to open windows into other worlds and that let the Spectres in. The people from Cittagazze learned to steal from other worlds because nobody lived long enough to build a society of their own. The reason for this is that the philosophers carelessly left many windows open, so allowing all sorts of trouble in from other worlds, along with other creatures like coalesced Dust, or angels.

Meanwhile, Lyra returns to twentieth-century Oxford to see Mary Malone, but finds the police waiting for her. They trick her into revealing that she knows Will, who naturally is wanted by them, but she flees only to be given a lift in a Rolls Royce by the dubious Sir Charles Latrom. He steals her divining instrument, the alethiometer. Lyra slips back to Cittagazze and brings back Will, and together they call on the man's house. He agrees to return the instrument if they find a certain knife that is kept in the Torre degli Angeli. Will and Lyra go to this tower and find a young madman who has stolen the knife from the old guardian. They fight the young man and obtain the knife, but Will loses two fingers in the process. This incidentally qualifies him to become the official bearer of the subtle knife. The old guardian teaches Will how to use the knife to open and close windows. He does so by using a mind abandonment technique reminiscent of *Star Wars*. The old man then commits suicide before the Spectres get to him.

Will and Lyra revisit Sir Charles' house to re-obtain the alethiometer by cutting a window into his world. There they make an interesting discovery: Sir Charles is actually from Lyra's world. His other name is Lord Boreal and he is Mrs Coulter's lover, and she's there in Will's Oxford with him. They overhear him tell Mrs Coulter that Cittagazze is the crossroads to all the worlds, but that Lord Asriel's blasting of a barrier between the worlds has upset the dozen or so known windows into the millions of worlds. They also learn that Lord Boreal is a government spy and that everyone is looking for windows into other worlds. They hear that Will's father was someone who probably knew the location of a window and went through it, which explains why the government officials were so interested in him.

Will and Lyra snatch the alethiometer from under the noses of Lord Boreal and Mrs Coulter and escape into Cittagazze. There they are attacked by the children, but are rescued by the witches, who then attempt, unsuccessfully, to brew a potion and make a magic spell to heal Will's wounded fingers. Will reflects on his experience of other children and the way they made fun of his demented mother, and concludes that children are as capable of evil as grown-ups.

Towards the end of the third volume, Mary Malone deduces that the philosophers of the Guild of the Torre degli Angeli, the owners of the subtle knife, have been careless and not closed the windows they have opened. So Dust has been leaking out of the wounds the subtle knife has made in nature.

However, the big flow of Dust that she can see through her amber spyglass is caused by something greater, and although matter itself, because of its love of Dust, is trying to stem the flow, it can't be stopped. This fully persuades her that she must play the part of the serpent and tempt Will and Lyra. Having done so, the flow of Dust stops, but all is not well. With all these windows left open the Spectres can have free rein to attack people, and it turns out that every time a window is opened, it creates another Spectre, which grows by feeding on Dust and daemons – hence their attacking adults who have Dust. That's why people become zombies.

The only answer is to close up every single window to stop Dust escaping and to stop Spectres from moving around or even being created. It's a big task, but not impossible if you possess the subtle knife. It has the power not only to open windows but also to close them, and here's the twist. Unfortunately, people cannot live long in another world because it drains the life out of them, and they have to return to their own world to recharge their batteries, so to speak. That leaves Will and Lyra with their tragic choice. Closing up every single window will mean either living together in one world or another, in which case one of them will die young, or they must separate for ever. Heartbroken, they choose, with the help of an angel called Xaphania, to close all the openings except for the one that will allow a way out from the place of the dead for the ghosts to become one with nature. Finally and tragically they part, and Will shatters the subtle knife.

He had done this before accidentally when trying to use the knife. His attention and emotions had wavered when he thought of his mother, and the knife broke. It was reforged by the armoured bear, Iorek Byrnison. Now he shatters it by thinking of Lyra, and so ends the possibility of any more windows being opened. If perhaps the windows represent imagination, does that mean the end of imagination? If so, it would mark a most depressing end to human creativity.

Paradigm shift

We should not, of course, automatically assume that the big bang is necessarily the way the universe originated. It isn't a theological issue since the theory neither proves nor disproves the existence of God. The Bible in any case says very little about the mechanics of creation since its message is aimed at a much wider audience than a few specialised Westernised scientists living in the twenty-first century, and it addresses far bigger themes than those allowed to their mental processes. Perhaps that's why it simply declares, 'In the beginning God created the heavens and the earth' (Genesis 1:1) and since 'the heavens declare the glory of God; the skies proclaim the work of his hands' (Psalm 19:1), the writers spend no time searching around for traces of God in the cosmos. The entire set-up proclaims loudly and clearly, from the macro to the micro, that there is a living and loving intelligence behind the universe and those who deny it are for reasons of perversity and prejudice like those who cannot see the wood for the trees.

The question mark over the big bang theory is more to do with the paradigms or assumed models through which we perceive and interpret the world around us. Often these paradigms are influenced by our latest technology. The ancient Greeks were fascinated by geometry and architecture, so they came up with a geometric interpretation of the universe. Later, when navigation developed, the clock became all important and unsurprisingly we used it as our new paradigm, the clockwork universe. This model lasted until Albert Einstein, who not only challenged the reliability of the clocks but laid the foundations for the nuclear bomb, and provided us with the big bang paradigm.

None of these paradigms has provided us with an adequate or complete explanation of the universe and in many ways the three mentioned are all of them derivatives of a non-personal deterministic model. It will be interesting to see what we make of our latest technological breakthroughs. Will the genetic revolution give us a more organic model of the universe – matter shaped in a manner that begets life? Or will the information revolution take us even further? The universe as information invites the possibility of an informer. Maybe we will have to take intelligence, personality and relationship into account and that might lead us to treat God as a legitimate part of science rather than a distraction from science. Philip Pullman with his Shadow particles of consciousness may after all be going in the right direction, of the devil's party or no, even though his version of pantheism is inadequate and he still has a way to travel!

Biblical cosmology does recognise parallel worlds or spheres, beginning with God himself in a tripartite intrinsic unity distinct from the created universe. Then we have early on that admittedly difficult reference to the Nephilim, which may suggest sexual congress between human women and some kind of fallen angelic beings not of earthly creation (Genesis 6:4). In the New Testament, Paul refers either to himself or to a close friend being caught up into the third heaven (2 Corinthians 12:2–4). It is akin to the apostle John's mystical experience of being in the Spirit on the Lord's day and seeing a door opened into heaven (Revelation 1:10; 4:1).

Cast in powerful and vivid imagery, the latter reference reveals to us a world very different from our own but maybe suggesting a reality where the laws operate differently. Be that as it may, we are given a glimpse of the realm to which Jesus ascended when he departed from the disciples after his resurrection and a cloud took him out of their sight (Acts 1:9).

Back in the 1960s John Robinson argued that this language no longer fitted a post-Copernican world (though it had apparently served well enough from the sixteenth century until 1960!),[3] and tried to redefine it as mystical experience – an experience that most people felt wasn't worth having. But why shouldn't Jesus lift off the ground and disappear into the clouds if that was just his way of transferring from one realm to another in a manner that would make sense to his onlookers? It is unwarranted to decide that it couldn't be historically true just because a later generation had a different paradigm for what they meant by up and down.

The other realm to which the New Testament refers is the one the apostle Paul called the heavenlies, commonly translated as 'heavenly places'. This is a realm of spiritual conflict, where the authority of Christ is exercised insofar as Christians believe themselves to be seated with Christ in those heavenly places and also where Satan, the prince of the power of the air, has influence: 'Our struggle is not against flesh and blood, but against the rulers, against the authorities, against the powers of this dark world and against the spiritual forces of evil in the heavenly realms' (Ephesians 6:12). These forces are bent on destruction and lurk behind the socio-political systems of the world, as in the book of Revelation where John understands Rome to be the great idolatrous harlot. What goes on in one realm has implications for the other – a thought that Philip Pullman should perhaps be comfortable with!

---

[3] Nicolaus Copernicus, born: 19 February 1473 in Torun, Poland; died: 24 May 1543 in Frombork, Poland.

Since quantum mechanics makes possible the idea of parallel worlds actually existing, though perhaps with very different laws and characteristics to this one, why should not heaven and for that matter hell already exist as realities? Could not the new heavens and the new earth already be in existence, just waiting for the return of Christ, or will his return perhaps catalyse them into being? After all, Jesus said that he would go to prepare a place for his people. He also promised to come back for them and take them to be with him in this new world. Maybe it's already there in a different dimension (John 14:1–3), much as the apostle Paul spoke of the existence of a Jerusalem that is above, the mother of all the free people of faith (Galatians 4:26). These are speculative interpretations, of course, but serve as a reminder that we in a postmodern generation no longer limit reality to the rigid constraints of Enlightenment materialism, and those Bible writers may have been onto something after all with their own subtle knife.

4

Heavenly Deception

TRUTH AND FALSEHOOD AND HOW TO TELL THE DIFFERENCE

Pontius Pilate infamously and ironically asked that epitome of truth, Jesus of Nazareth, 'What is truth?' (John 18:38). We might add, 'Who can we trust to tell the truth?' And to that, 'What reliable means shall we use to ascertain the truth?' Questions about truth and falsehood, and the means of verification, run as a subtext throughout *His Dark Materials*. It is complicated by the fact that none of the main characters seems capable of telling the truth with any degree of consistency. The heroine Lyra is an eponymously expert liar; likewise her sidekick, Will. Lord Asriel and Mrs Coulter use deceit continually in their pursuit of power. Mary Malone is too flawed a character to be trustworthy. The church is deemed corrupt beyond measure, and God himself is a total deceiver!

It's all far removed from the old moral adage that it is better to tell the truth. Expediency is everything. None of the characters makes a good role model for children, least of all the hero and heroine, and that is a point that responsible parents and teachers might wish to bear in mind. It would not be so bad if Pullman were simply reversing the roles of the good guys and the bad guys: sometimes we can gain an insight into the nature of good and evil by looking at it from a reverse perspective, just as the negative of a photograph can reveal detail that we might otherwise miss. Yet this simplicity is absent from *His Dark Materials*; it is so filled with ambiguity and subtle deceits that in this case reverse is perverse and we are reminded of Isaiah's caution: 'Woe to those who call evil good and good evil, who put darkness for light and light for darkness, who put bitter for sweet and sweet for bitter' (Isaiah 5:20).

This is blatantly apparent when it comes to Pullman's portrayal of God and the church. It would be nice to think that *His Dark Materials* is tackling only a parody of God in one particular world, but the unmitigated and uncompromising antipathy towards God, and the explicit use of his names drawn from the Bible in our world, allows no such latitude. Likewise, the church is presented in such a way that you would easily conclude that not just in Lyra's world, but in all possible worlds, it is an unqualified evil. We shall return to these matters in later chapters. Suffice it to note that the trilogy will do little to assist those who believe that children need to learn the difference between light and darkness, good and evil, truth and untruth, without which socialisation and civilisation are impossible. Those raised in a sea of relativism and deceit become deceivers and themselves deceived. If nobody can trust anybody, then we lose the possibility of society.

Divining the truth

Truth and deception come to the fore in the manner by which the central characters seek guidance. Carrying the plot along is a supra-natural technology of occult divination, and since it is so commended in the story we are entitled to examine the merits of this form of truth discernment.

At the beginning of the story in *Northern Lights*, the influential and charismatic Mrs Coulter, with her fierce monkey daemon, comes to Jordan College. She entrances Lyra at the first meeting and it is agreed that she should take over Lyra's education to groom the girl in the social and intellectual arts and graces that the scholars of Jordan College have not been able to give her. Just

before she leaves the college, and without Mrs Coulter's knowledge, the Master gives Lyra a solid gold instrument adorned with
dials and symbols and needles that can be used for divination. It's
call an alethiometer – a truth meter.[1]

When the gyptians decide to venture north to rescue the children
captured by the Gobblers, Lyra begins to practise with the
alethiometer. She quickly proves to be an adept and is able to
predict accurately the death of a gyptian spy. This persuades the
gyptian leaders, Lord John Farr and Fador Coran, to take Lyra with
them, realising in spite of the dangers to herself just how useful
she might be to the expedition. It is her use of the alethiometer on
the way to Bolvanger that uncovers what she thinks is a ghost in a
village but which turns out to be a boy whose daemon has been
removed from him.

Later on Lyra uses the alethiometer to discover that Mrs Coulter
is coming to invade Svalbard to kill Lord Asriel because she fears
that he will build a bridge to the city in the sky. This presents us
with a problem because when Mrs Coulter does melodramatically
meet Asriel they seem to be the best of friends and he even invites
her to go with him. Furthermore it is Lyra's journey to Svalbard, in
the mistaken belief that Lord Asriel needs the alethiometer, that
leads to the death of her friend Roger. The truth meter appears not
to be telling the truth. Or are we to conclude that the alethiometer
deliberately lied to get her to sacrifice Roger, so that later on she
could go to the place of the dead to apologise to Roger and in so
doing rescue all the ghosts? But that really is a *deus ex machina*[2]
and a poor device for an author to use, to say nothing of the
capricious and callous nature of such a god.

The alethiometer is not an objective scientific machine; it is an
instrument used for occult divination and as with all such artefacts,
the interpretation of the symbols depends as much upon the
character, personality and knowledge of the user as on the symbols

---

[1] Greek: *aletheia + metron.*
[2] Literally, god out of a machine; a god introduced artificially into a play to resolve
the plot.

themselves. We may then question how trustworthy can be the perceptions of someone for whom lying is a way of life – although as Lyra's character develops she does learn a measure of honesty, if not of truth. Is Lyra not herself deceived or indeed deceiving others, consciously or otherwise, when she uses this instrument? The fact that she predicts certain things that subsequently happen proves nothing. Merely on the law of averages some of the nonsense written in daily horoscopes will come to pass – or at least appear to – in the experience of those who read the stuff. It hardly constitutes scientific proof or validates divination.

Since so many people make so many decisions based upon Lyra's interpretation of her alethiometer, we're entitled to ask whether the entire tale is not one great foolish quest based on deception and merely circumstantially giving what appears to be a good outcome; that is, the apparent end of the flow of Dust.

Dust is the secret of the alethiometer, for it is operated not just by Lyra from her side, but by the consciousness that is Dust, or angelic consciousness. This is, of course, fallen angelic consciousness, though fallen means good in this book. Why should we believe that this Dust is telling the truth? On what grounds should we think that it represents good consciousness? Why not bad? Perhaps Lyra, unable to discern truth from falsehood because of her flawed character, is being manipulated by an alien intelligence that is far from good for the human race.

The same uncertainty arises when Lyra encounters Mary Malone. She convinces Malone to let her try the detection machine, the Cave, by using the alethiometer to prove that Malone used to be a nun. She is very successful and it becomes apparent that the computer works like her alethiometer; both are interactive occult computers, one from a mechanical age and the other from the electronic age. But just as Lyra is hardly qualified to discern the truth, Mary Malone is anything but an objective scientist. Her own inner life is deeply damaged by her quite unnecessary rejection of the Christian faith in favour of what she thought was love. She had also decided that science and religion were incompatible – a patent nonsense, as any decent theistic scientist will tell us.[3]

Having abandoned prayer and the Bible, Mary Malone now turns to I Ching, an old Chinese form of occult divination, using sticks and a reference book called *The Book of Changes*. It turns out that this is operated by Dust as well. I Ching is supposed to be the way that Chinese fortune tellers communicate with Shadow particles, Dust, dark matter, angels in waiting, whatever, when they perform their occult divination. On what grounds should we believe that this is any more true or reliable than her former Christian means of prayer and the Bible? Dust tells Malone that she must now play the part of the serpent. Perhaps she is a good candidate; her objectivity is suspect and her psyche is damaged. In our world, hearing aliens speaking to you through your computer telling you that you are to act the devil usually means you need time off work and possibly some tablets!

The church might be considered by some to be the repository of truth, but Pullman's medieval parody allows no such possibility. The church is deceived and deceiving, and should we feel this is unfair and ask why the apparent liars (i.e. the church) should not be telling the truth and the apparent truth tellers be liars, then we will be directed towards its obvious cruelty and malice. If, as Jesus said, it is by their fruits that we know them, then it is clearly rotten to the core (Matthew 7:20).

We must allow Pullman to be in charge of his own universe, of course, and none of this would matter if this were just a tale. After all, there's nothing wrong in having a book in which every character is corrupt. The credibility problem arises insofar as all this duplicity and deception and dubious fortune telling serves the polemical nature of the story. It is hard to read *His Dark Materials*

---

[3] Typical theistic scientists include people like Johannes Kepler, Nicolaus Copernicus, Galileo Galilei, Blaise Pascal, William Harvey, Robert Boyle, Isaac Newton, Carolus Linnaeus, William Herschel, Samuel Morse, Charles Babbage, Michael Faraday, James Joule, James Maxwell, John Napier, George Boole, Gregor Mendel, Louis Pasteur, Joseph Lister, Allan Sandage, Francis Collins – to name but a few.

without feeling that we are meant to believe its underlying message: down with the kingdom of heaven; up with the republic of heaven! And here's where the behavioural test cuts both ways. Can we, for example, trust Will and Lyra with their blatant lying and their underage sexual engagement? Would we rely on the witches, one of whom vindictively murders Will's father John? Are we meant to excuse the violence and arrogance of Lord Asriel and Mrs Coulter because they are fulfilling the supposedly good task of destroying God and the church? In any other context it would be known as selective morality.

With so much duplicity, why shouldn't the Dust that communicates with Malone be truly bad angels, wanting to maintain just a different form of evil and, finding her a susceptible candidate, seduce her into believing she has some grandiose role to play in history that will actually turn out to serve another malevolence? And since all Dust is angels, including the angels on the side of God, how would we sort out one Dust from the other? Such are the problems of moral relativism! As the Roman Catholic philosopher Thomas Aquinas (1225–74) said of his own work, though in his case without justification, '*mihi videtur ut pavia*' ('It all seems like dust').

Is there anyone there?

Since divination plays such a central part in *His Dark Materials* and might appear commendable to younger readers, it will be as well to make a few observations.

The first problem with divination is this: how do you know that your source of information, or your medium for that matter, is actually telling the truth? Character, in the real world and in *His Dark Materials*, is an insufficient guide because all characters are to a greater or lesser extent flawed. Events coming to pass are seldom of a degree of accuracy or consistency to constitute anything like proof, and sincerity may just mean misguided zeal.

More serious a concern is the amassed evidence of pastoral and psychological experience that demonstrates the confusion and fear that comes upon so many people who engage in this kind of occult activity. Far from releasing people into peace and security, it so often does the very opposite – and for many, trying to know the future becomes a morbid obsession that leads them into ever deeper bondage.

Pullman suggests that divination is a way of communicating with Dust; in other words he wants to answer the question 'Is there anybody there?' with a yes. Of course, his Dust is wholly good – rebel angels that are bent on destroying divine deception. The reality may be somewhat different. When people open themselves up to Ouija boards, astrology, divination and the like, global evidence suggests that they may expose themselves to manipulation by external forces that are actually malign in their intent, and that is why they create such subtle and often destructive psychological bondages. It may not be politically correct among certain of the Western intelligentsia, and we need to detach ourselves from the more lurid depictions, yet most of the world today, as with Jesus himself, recognises the sad reality of demonisation. That is why Paul could sum up Jesus' ministry thus: 'God anointed Jesus of Nazareth with the Holy Spirit and power … he went around doing good and healing all who were under the power of the devil, because God was with him' (Acts 10:38).[4]

---

[4] Jesus treated demons as a reality, and he did so as a man universally recognised as the greatest moral and spiritual teacher ever – quite apart from his astounding self-sacrifice for the human race. Some have suggested that he simply accommodated to the popular beliefs of his day, or even that he believed in demons because he was a child of his times, whereas humans today in their enlightened age have seen these manifestations to be no more than morbid psychoses, curable through counselling and behaviour-modifying drugs. This is to assume that the Enlightenment worldview, so successful in the realm of the physical sciences, is somehow an objective tool for analysing the human psyche. Many of us would question whether the 'man as a machine' approach can ever do justice to the complexity of what it means to be human. We are creatures of spirit and it isn't unreasonable to suppose that there could be alien and malign intelligences intent on wreaking destruction on the souls of the vulnerable.

This is not to say that every problem is demonic by any means, any more than to suggest that every sneeze heralds bubonic plague – but some sneezes just might. Nor has casting out demons, or exorcism, anything to do with the fervid imaginations of Hollywood film directors.

With so many living in secret fear because of their superstitious belief that somehow their fate, or their destiny, is in the hands of the predictions of their fortune teller, divination of this kind is, to say the least, unwise. And if we want to speak about exploitation for vested interests, then there are tens of thousands of charlatans who are making money from the desire of the gullible to have some certainty about their future. Pagan divination has brought anything but peace and security to human society.

It is worth noting in passing that the occult world to which the Christian gospel first came received the message gladly – and without any physical or political coercion – simply because they discovered in Christ a glorious liberation from their slavery to the manipulative and destructive world of their pagan religions, which is why the apostle Paul could say with all confidence, 'It is for freedom that Christ has set us free' (Galatians 5:1). When the Ephesian pagans received the gospel, they burned their occult books and artefacts, not because of some imposed censorship by a dictatorial church, but because they were prisoners who had been set free and were only too glad to destroy the shackles of their former bondage.

Character guidance

The issue of character is important when it comes to whom, or even how, we consult when we have to make life choices. Genuine New Testament faith focuses upon freedom in Christ, and his followers can find their way through life because of their direct spiritual connection to the one person who could say with utter integrity that he was 'the way and the truth and the life' (John 14:6). Jesus was tempted just like everyone else, but he never sinned. Even his most acute critics, those legalistic religious experts, couldn't wrong foot him in terms of his conduct or behaviour – except, of course, when they by deceit decided to destroy him for fear of his penetrating words. Jesus was the man of ultimate integrity and there was no expediency or economy with the truth in his life at all. He told it compassionately but clearly, and he lived it blamelessly.[5] That makes him trustworthy.

Another factor in a biblical approach to guidance has to do with the leading of the Holy Spirit and here, though we may wish to reject Lyra's occultism and mistrust her ability to know the truth, we may have some sympathy for her, for she at least comes to recognise that guidance must be based upon more than mere rationalism. It requires communication with an intelligence beyond her own and the trusting exercise of an evident gift. Likewise the Christian needs more than secular wisdom, and certainly more than ecclesiastical diktat, to find the way through life. Along with our need for the Bible is the need to exercise the genuine gifts of the Holy Spirit.

In this we find the church in our own world to be often lacking. The New Testament charismata, the gifts of the Spirit, lie dormant in many congregations and that has left a void which the New Age movement has been quick to fill. Even those churches that do recognise such gifts often restrict their operation to church services and then bemoan the local occult shop that has set up at the point of people's need. Pullman's emphasis on Dust as a consciousness may fall far short of what we mean by the Holy Spirit, but if he reminds us of the importance of the Holy Spirit in our search for wisdom, meaning and guidance, then once more he may unwittingly serve the purpose of God rather than the devil's party.

Those gifts of the Spirit address the need we have for wisdom and proper guidance in the conduct of our affairs: words of knowledge, words of wisdom, dreams and visions, and prophecy itself are all tools for spiritual discernment to assist people in the complex business of living.

Caution is needed, however. If we object to Lyra being an autonomous expert, why not level the same charge at the ordinary imperfect Christian? This is where the corporateness, the fellow-

---

[5] Pullman has little time for the church, but he does express a respect for Jesus.

ship of the body of Christ, comes into play, especially in the context of a set of local relationships based upon mutual trust, humility and integrity.

The Quaker model is one such outworking of what this means. In the stillness, an entire gathering may come to a remarkable unity in their perception of the will of God, based not on persuasive rhetoric, let alone dogma, but simply upon listening to what the Spirit of God is saying to the church. In his book *Beyond Majority Rule*[6] Michael J. Sheeran finds this approach far more akin to the New Testament than so many of our notions of ecclesiastical hierarchy, or our often polarised democratic church meetings. Nevertheless, he observes that many other churches outside of the Quaker movement operate in much the same manner, particularly when they pray together.

The biblical Christian finds truth rooted in a Person. That Person is revealed through a trustworthy record that tells it like it is. The Bible reveals a God who is holy and true and pure in all his ways and whose laws expressed in nature, in cosmology, in the way the universe functions, demonstrate the fundamental integrity of his character by their very reliability and consistency, and make life and science possible. This revelation isn't given capriciously, as with the gods of Mount Olympus, nor manipulatively like the gods of animistic superstition, but out of a heart of unutterable love. This knowledge of God allows people to see life as it really is, but to do so without Pilate's cynicism or despair. It doesn't make people hide their heads in the sand; instead it provides them with the strength and clarity of purpose to work for the protection of the innocent and the vulnerable and to seek to build a better society. It provides the moral waymarks that enable people to live their lives with integrity and constructiveness and with a due care for one another. It provides them with the moral strength to resist the subtle wiles of the devil, whether those are manifested in political

---

[6] Michael J. Sheeran, *Beyond Majority Rule* (Philadelphia Yearly Meeting of the Religious Society of Friends, 1996).

deceit, facetious promises or the lures of the wicked, and it does so through the immediate presence and guidance of the Holy Spirit. For many millions throughout the world this is a more reliable choice for life direction than some supposed universal consciousness of Dust operating through a dubious truth meter.

5

Angels, Witches and Shamans

HEAVENLY BODIES AND THE DOUBTFUL MERITS OF A HOLE IN THE HEAD

Philip Pullman freely acknowledges the influence of John Milton's *Paradise Lost* on his own work; indeed, in many ways *His Dark Materials* is, in part, a retelling of the classic, albeit with the roles of the good guys and the bad reversed. To understand where Pullman is coming from we need to know a little about Milton himself and *Paradise Lost*.

John Milton was born in London in 1608 and was well educated at St Paul's school and Christ's College, Cambridge. He lived through the time of the Civil War between the royalist supporters of Charles I and the Parliamentarians (1640–48). Milton identified himself with the Puritan cause and actively supported the Parliamentarians, going so far as to write in support of the execution of Charles I. With the demise of Cromwell and the restoration of the monarchy under Charles II in 1660, Milton retired from public life and was fortunate not to suffer reprisals. Although by now blind, he wrote *Paradise Lost* in 1667, dying in 1674.

Milton was a strange mixture of the austere and the sensual, and this is reflected in his work. He married three times but was an undoubted male chauvinist. Nor did Milton conform to the then current orthodoxy of the Protestants, abandoning the Calvinist doctrine of predestination and tending towards an Arian view of God that refused the Son equal status with the Father. Significantly, he believed that matter was a divine principle and endowed by God with the principle of life and thought; and as a consequence the body and soul in man are one, not two. This position seeks to avoid the problem of Greek dualism, but leaves the difficulty of what happens when the body dies or is killed. Does the soul also then die? Milton seemed to accept mortalism, the notion that at death all men and women die to be revived again only at the last judgement. This notion of 'the long sleep' runs counter to the promise Jesus made to the dying thief, as well as other scriptures already noted. It is more akin to a limited Old Testament perspective, and in many ways Milton's view of God is more dominated by that than by the New Testament.

John Milton was arguably more humanist than Christian, believing in the importance of reason and the power of humanity to recover itself after a lapse. He had sympathies with the Quakers, believing that the spirit which is given to us is a more certain guide than Scripture (*de doctrina christiana*). William Blake was later to suggest that Milton was of the devil's party but did not know it, and certainly his portrayal of Satan suggests more than a little sympathy for the character.

Mixing fact and fiction is always a tricky business and even more so when we mix theology with fiction. The vivid imagery of fictional writing and the demands of the medium tend rather to warp the theology. Unfortunately, people find it all too easy to accept the fictional paradigm and then unconsciously interpret their theology in the light of it. *Paradise Lost* itself draws only loosely and erroneously on the Bible and extrapolates ideas far beyond the Scriptures. For example, it is tenuous to suggest that there was ever a created world of angels before the creation of our planet, or even that there was some kind of war in heaven predating the earth. Yet, thanks to *Paradise Lost*, this is almost inevitably the interpretation that Bible readers put on those passages that describe the heavenly battle and the fall of Satan. Similarly, as a child of his time he reflected the known cosmology of the scientific establishment and fitted his characters into their clockwork universe, but endowed them with classical conceptions of angels with wings and the like – rather reminiscent of the stylised film *Flash Gordon*, with its curious mix of feathered wings and spacecraft.

Angel dust

The creation of angels is never described in detail in the Bible; we know neither precisely when nor how. Perhaps the nearest we get to it is in the poetic language of Job: 'Where were you when I laid the earth's foundation ... while the morning stars sang together and all the angels shouted for joy?' (Job 38:4,7). As for feathered wings, no angel in the Bible possesses such appendages. In fact, although they often appear in supernatural forms, equally they may turn up in such naturally human forms that it is possible for the hospitable believer to entertain angels unawares (Hebrews 13:2). While Joshua encounters the sense of the numinous in his angelic visitation (Joshua 5:13–15), Abraham and Sarah's encounter is almost homespun in its ordinariness (Genesis 18:1–15). The only place where supernatural beings have wings is in the presence of God, as with the seraphim in Isaiah 6 and the four living creatures in Revelation 5. Whether these creatures exist literally, as described, in a parallel universe, or whether it is simply symbolic language to indicate heavenliness and speed is, of course, a matter of interpretation, not to say speculation.

Belief in angels is a ubiquitous human phenomenon and interestingly on the increase in the West, with a mass of evidence from perfectly sane people – including the present author – indicating encounters with such beings. Jesus was obviously at home with their existence, and that was not simply a matter of his accommodating to the popular beliefs of his time; they played a significant role in his earthly life.

The Bible lays the foundation for both Milton's and Pullman's writings in that it records a division in the angelic ranks and a fall from grace of a significant number, headed by the devil. Contrary to Milton it is likely that the fall of Satan took place after the creation was completed, because God pronounced on the seventh day of creation that everything was good – though arguably that might not include heavenly beings. However, the prophet Ezekiel, speaking about the King of Tyre but clearly extrapolating to the power behind the king, i.e. Satan, says:

> You were the model of perfection, full of wisdom and perfect in beauty. You were in Eden, the garden of God ... You were anointed as a guardian cherub, for so I ordained you. You were on the holy mount of God; you walked among the fiery stones. You were blameless in your ways from the day you were created till wickedness was found in you. (Ezekiel 28:12–15)

This is backed up by the prophet Isaiah:

> How you have fallen from heaven, O morning star, son of the dawn! You have been cast down to the earth, you who once laid low the nations! You said in your heart, 'I will ascend to heaven; I will raise my throne above the stars of God; I will sit enthroned on the mount of assembly on the utmost heights of the sacred mountain. I will ascend above the tops of the clouds; I will make myself like the Most High.' (Isaiah 14:12–14)

It seems evident that the most exalted guardian angel over the Garden of Eden grew proud of his position and, desiring the place of God himself, fell from grace. He then seductively and malevolently set about corrupting the pinnacle of God's creation by tempting Eve and then Adam to join him in rebellion against God. Having sold out to him, and because of his original status, they came under his power. Jesus rightly described Satan as the Prince of this world, a situation that remained true until Jesus himself was pronounced King of kings and Lord of lords and the rightful heir to the nations.

The other significant passage that 'war in heaven' writers draw on is Revelation 12, a passage that continues its influence even in the sci-fi movie *Terminator 2*. The highly symbolic language presents us with a pregnant woman about to give birth and a seven-headed, ten-horned enormous red dragon prepared to devour the child the moment it is born. The child and the woman are saved, but then

> there was war in heaven. Michael and his angels fought against the dragon, and the dragon and his angels fought back. But he was not strong enough, and they lost their place in heaven. The great dragon was hurled down – that ancient serpent called the devil, or Satan, who leads the whole world astray. He was hurled to the earth, and his angels with him. (Revelation 12:7–9)

Clearly this passage also indicates that the war took place after the creation of the world. The numbers of angels are symbolic, but the outcome was 2–1 in favour of God!

It would seem that the fallen angels became demons – in the biblical sense and not as Philip Pullman when describing the animal souls of people – and they seem to form a crude hierarchy. This appears to be the case with the unfallen angels too, but it is not developed to the degree that Milton would have it in *Paradise Lost*.

Two angels come on the scene at the end of *The Subtle Knife*. These are of course coalesced Dust, angel dust. Their names are Baruch and Balthamos, and they are passionately in love with each other in a manner that suggests they are homosexuals. Pullman calls his angels *Bene Elim*, which is Hebrew for 'sons of the gods', perhaps referring to those in Genesis 6 who had intercourse with the daughters of men. For the record, when Jesus spoke of heaven as a place where marriage was superseded by something even better, he said that people become like angels, neither marrying nor being given in marriage, which indicates that angels do not enjoy sexual love, having no need of it (Matthew 22:30).

The Amber Spyglass opens with Lyra lying unconscious in a Himalayan cave as the drugged prisoner of her mother. Will, having left his dead father, refuses to go to Lord Asriel until he has found Lyra. Balthamos, a somewhat effete and waspish character, is peeved at having to accompany Will in his search for the girl. Baruch nonetheless ventures ahead and discovers Lyra's whereabouts, when suddenly they are attacked by a being called the Metatron. This is apparently the regent appointed by the Authority. Balthamos explains that the Authority, who claimed to be God, wasn't God at all; instead he was an angel just like Baruch and Balthamos. The Authority just happened to be the first angel, but like the rest he was formed out of Dust, 'and Dust is only a name for what happens when matter begins to understand itself. Matter loves matter. It seeks to know more about itself, and Dust is formed.'[1] Lest we doubt that Pullman is referring to the God of the Jews and later of the Christians in this blasphemy, he spells it out through Balthamos: 'The Authority, God, the Creator, the Lord, Yahweh, El, Adonai, the King, the Father, the Almighty.' No ambiguity there, then!

Apart from the anti-Semitic and anti-Christian sentiments, the references to Dust and matter remind us of the oxymoron referred to earlier and tempt us to think that it is all complete balderdash! It's not helped by a further and unresolved piece of information thrown in by Balthamos: the Authority was the first angel, but claimed to have created all those who appeared subsequently, 'but it was a lie. One of those who came later was wiser than he was, and she found out the truth, so he banished her. We serve her still.'[2] Who is she? If it's Mrs Coulter, then she seems a thoroughly unlikely and quite distasteful character for the role. The only other real candidate is a naked winged angel named Xaphania, who turns up at the end of the story to ask Will how to close the openings that the knife makes. But it's never quite clear.

---

[1] *TAS*, 33.
[2] *TAS*, 34.

The angel Baruch reaches Lord Asriel, but is mortally wounded. He manages with his dying breath to tell Asriel that the Authority has delegated power to an angel called Metatron. Metatron wants to turn the clouded mountain – known as the Chariot – where he lives into an engine of war and set up a permanent inquisition in every world, run directly from the kingdom. His first campaign will be to destroy Asriel's republic. This Metatron – a nasty piece of work – turns out originally to have been Enoch, the son of Jared, the son of Mahalelel, and Baruch was his brother.

The earliest reference to Enoch is in Genesis 5. Far from being an evil tyrant, Enoch was a good man who 'walked with God'. So much so that he seems to have disappeared off the earth without going through death. This is confirmed by the New Testament writer to the Hebrews, who describes Enoch as a man of true faith (Hebrews 11:5–6). This Enoch was also a prophet who spoke of coming judgement (Jude 14–15).

However, Pullman's ideas seem to have been culled from the Book of Enoch, an apocryphal work penned in the second century BC and filled with fantastical imagery, including mountains in the sky and angels, and incidentally a character named Azazel – maybe the source for Lord Asriel.

The only men called Baruch in the Bible are Baruch the son of Neriah, scribe to Jeremiah (Jeremiah 32:12), and Baruch, son of Col-Hozeh, a returned exile living in the time of Nehemiah (Nehemiah 11:5). Neither by any stretch of the imagination could have been the brother of Enoch.

Sexy witches

Apart from angels there are witches galore in *His Dark Materials*. Following the now predictable pattern of the story, the witches are good and the church persecutes them. Pullman's witches are a separate clannish society that have relatively little to do with the affairs of human beings, except when they want sex. Pullman describes his witches romantically as very long-lived, beautiful, slender-limbed females, scarcely clad in shreds of black cloth, riding on their branches of cloud pine and fighting battles with bows and arrows.[3] They have very little interest in mortal men, but when they want children, they seduce a man and fall passionately in love with him – though that love is always tinged with sadness, because men do not live as long as witches. If a child born to a witch is male, then the child is a mere human being, but if the child is female, then automatically she is a witch and that is why the witches are only female.

The notion of the succubus, the witch or demon, having intercourse with a man (the male equivalent is the incubus) is sometimes tracked back to Genesis 6 and the *Bene Elim*, where it could be construed that some form of angelic union of a sexual nature took place with the daughters of men. The offspring of these unions were giants and it provoked God to limit the life of humans to 120 years because the world had become a place of unimaginable wickedness. God was grieved to the point of regretting his great work of creating people in his own image who would love him freely. It laid the foundation for the flood and the story of Noah.

This particular sexual appetite of the witches in *His Dark Materials* has a pivotal bearing on the story. Will's father, John Parry, is killed by a vengeful witch just as he meets his son, because he chose to remain faithful to his wife and refused to have intercourse with the witch. The marital fidelity expressed here is to be commended and perhaps it should be added that much psychological and spiritual damage can occur in those who engage in morbid sexual fantasies involving incubi and succubi.

In the first volume, when the gyptians arrive at Trolleshund in Lapland, they immediately seek out the consul of the witches. The

---

[3] Witches have visible daemons just as the humans do in Lyra's world, but with this difference: witches' daemons can travel considerable distances – a kind of soul travel reminiscent of so-called astral travel. Lyra and Will lose their daemons for a while after voluntarily giving them up to travel to the place of the dead. When towards the end of the story they are reunited with them, they are told that they have become as witches because their daemons can exist at a distance from them.

consul informs them that though the missing children are of no concern to witches, they know that they have been taken to a place in the northern hinterland called Bolvanger. The consul advises them that Tartar soldiers guard the place and that they would be wise to hire the services of Iorek Byrnison, the armoured bear. He also informs the gyptians that Lyra is the child whose coming has long been prophesied and that her divination skill is proof of this. Lyra correctly identifies which broomstick a certain witch named Serafina Pekkala used for her travels (nothing as crude as a besom broom, but rather poetically a spray of cloud pine), thus proving her to be the chosen one.

Although there are renegade witches, Serafina Pekkala and the queen of the witches, Ruta Skadi, side with Lord Asriel in his war against heaven. This decision is made at a witches' council where the queen of the witches warns that the Magisterium, the church, has always tried to suppress natural impulses, and if it can't, then it destroys them. She charges churches with castrating children and tells the witches that if a war comes they must fight on the side other than the church because of the evil nature of the church.

This idea that the church is opposed to feelings and particularly to sex is so yawningly predictable and erroneous as scarcely to be worth comment, but because the sexual theme runs through *His Dark Materials* in this vein we need to set the record in order. Philosophically, it was the Greeks who were opposed to sex, not the Hebrews or the Christians. It all arose out of the Platonic ideal of a spiritual world wherein lay the true reality, and the earth being only a poor copy. It was a simple step from there to suggest that the physical impulses should be suppressed, or ignored and despised, in the pursuit of spirituality. This became a problem for those parts of the church that, in their philosophic desire to bring together Jerusalem and Athens, became infected with Platonism. Historically, and especially today, the vast majority of the church throughout the world roundly rejects the Platonic influence, and I have yet to come across a genuine biblical Christian who despises sex and pleasure because of their faith.

The fact that parts of the church embraced the Greek dualism between the earthly and the spiritual is down to a failure to apprehend the unity of the material and the spiritual implicit in the creation of humankind. Adam is of the dust of the ground but enlivened with the breath of God (Genesis 2:7). This perfect unity is re-expressed in the coming of Jesus: 'The Word [*Logos*] became flesh [*sarx*] and made his dwelling among us ... full of grace and truth' (John 1:14). In Jesus is found the perfect harmony and unity of the spiritual and the physical, and thus the affirmation of both. The divide between the two, with its attendant contradictions and tensions, is a problem for Greek philosophy, not Christian. This holism is characteristic of Jesus' life and teaching, and is followed through consistently in the writings of the apostles. So Paul, while deploring the sexual licence of pagan society, nonetheless insists that a husband and wife should render equally to one another their conjugal rights (1 Corinthians 7:3–5). It should be pointed out, however, that because of the anticipated troubles coming on the world, he indicated that those who had the gift would have less trouble by remaining unmarried and celibate, as he himself.

Striking the right balance between a proper enjoyment of God's good gifts and avoiding the excesses and perversions of the pagan world remains a challenge for a pilgrim people, but it is one that can be outworked healthily in every generation once we renounce the dualism of the Greeks and embrace a Christ-centred Hebrew–Christian worldview as our starting point.

The 'church is anti-sex' stance creates a logical inconsistency in *His Dark Materials*. The church is supposed to be opposed to sex because it's on the side of God, but the regent of God, this Metatron, otherwise known as Enoch, is portrayed as a man of prodigious sexual appetite, who had many wives and who cast Baruch out because of his homosexual love for Balthamos. Of course, there's no evidence in the Bible for any of this, but it does seem illogical that a randy regent of God should somehow produce a church that doesn't like sex!

The witches are obviously no friends of the church, and they can hardly be blamed when Mrs Coulter, a zealous servant of the church, personally tortures a witch in an effort to find out the truth about Lyra. That news inspires most clans of witches to side with Lord Asriel in his attempt to destroy the Authority. This is fair enough in the story but leaves us nonetheless with the predictable depiction of the wicked church persecuting witches, just to remind us of those dark days of the Inquisition and the later Protestant paranoia that led to witch-hunting. We might be forgiven for thinking that nothing else has happened in the past 2,000 years of the church's history!

What the pundits never make clear is the fact that not only were witch-hunts a thankfully short-lived and sporadic phenomenon, but they were inspired far less by ecclesiastical mandates than by the general paranoia that beset Western Europe. The same is true of the early American settlers. In both instances such practices arose as a panic-stricken attempt to handle disturbing economic events, widespread insecurity, disease, death, famine and war. It all combined to make a largely uneducated population suspicious of just about anybody. Indeed, it was very often genuine believers who were persecuted in these situations, rather than so-called witches. Even so, no one can defend that kind of behaviour, any more than one can defend the Inquisition. People who act in such a manner cannot be classed as true followers of Christ and no amount of ecclesiastical politics or sophistry can excuse such iniquities.

Arthur Miller's play, *The Crucible* (1953), though dishonest regarding the facts surrounding Salem, nevertheless has a good section on what he dubs daemonism. The term describes a paranoid situation where accusations begin to fly around and all kinds of people are accused of being on the devil's side. The phenomenon can affect a community to such an extent that the innocent are deemed to be the most guilty of all because they, by their outward innocence, are assumed to be deceitfully hiding their true sinister nature. So the only safe position to hold is that of an accuser. It leads to a hysteria of accusation that lasts until enough innocent blood has been shed and then cold realism seems to restore a sense of sanity, no doubt followed by sober regret for the entire episode.

What Miller was attacking were the McCarthy witch-hunts of the late 1940s and early 1950s, when American society became obsessed with a fear of communism. But the problem wasn't restricted to the USA. Soviet Russia and communist China – atheistic societies – persecuted many hundreds of thousands of people, including so-called witches, because they were looking for scapegoats to account for the failure of the ideology to deliver the goods. Singling out the church is at the least specious, but then it does merely reflect the standard prejudices of secular fundamentalism.

Those who want to defend the persecution of witches remind us that in the Old Testament theocracy, witchcraft was banned: 'Do not allow a sorceress to live' (Exodus 22:18). However, Moses did not have in mind harmless herbalists or lonely old women. It was those who blatantly and publicly sought to lead people into the prevailing paganism of the Canaanite gods that were the problem. In that society the witches referred to were guilty of child abuse, and child sacrifice and sexual perversion, often burning children alive. To understand the severity of the ban on witchcraft, we must grasp the fact that those targeted were child murderers and, according to the prevailing law, subject to the death penalty. Further, because the nation had entered a solemn covenant with God – blessing for obedience to the Ten Commandments and the ceremonial law, and cursing for disobedience – it was a very serious affair for them. The tragic and terrible experiences of conquest and exile demonstrated only too clearly the price of participating in this kind of witchcraft.

When we come to the New Testament we find the gospel spreading throughout a culture suffused with witchcraft and paganism. It is no longer a theocratic setting, and the gospel is offered to witches and to everyone else on equal terms. Witches can be saved, not by setting fire to them, but by inviting them to become followers of Christ, as many evidently did. We have already cited the case of Ephesus, where the witches and their followers voluntarily made a great bonfire of their occult books and artefacts.

Although the New Testament roundly rejects true witchcraft, there is no indication that the church would ever seek to persecute or kill witches. In fact, it has usually been the other way round, with the church most often on the receiving end of persecution – as it still is throughout the world.[4]

A holy priesthood

One can't help but feel sorry for Will's father John Parry, and for Will himself. After all, he discovers his long-lost dad, only tragically to find himself with a corpse on his hands.

John Parry found his way into Lyra's world through a window from twentieth-century England, but then couldn't get back. Resigned to his fate, he went to Berlin and became a professor, then later he became involved with the Tartars and had himself trepanned. The crude notion of a hole in the head was to let Dust access his personality more effectively. In an Oxford museum, trepanned skulls had more Dust around them, even though they were supposedly 30,000 years old.

Parry develops heightened consciousness; indeed, replete with rituals and ceremonies and mystic insights, he becomes a shaman. He takes a new name, Jopari, which resembles John Parry, his original name, and he is also known as Grumman. A mercenary balloonist, Lee Scoresby, is searching for him because Parry knows of an immensely powerful object that would help Lyra. This turns

---

[4] The book of Revelation ends with a warning that sorcery is among the many evils of the human race that ultimately separate people from God (Revelation 21:8). With the growing paganism of Western society and a significant populist return to witchcraft, the church, while not persecuting witches, nonetheless has a responsibility to offer them the gospel of Jesus Christ with a serious call to a changed lifestyle.

out to be the subtle knife. They eventually meet up, but find themselves in a gun battle, which kills Lee Scoresby. That, by the way, invokes the wrath of Iorek Byrnison, who has become a friend of Lee's, and it puts him and the bears firmly on the side of Lord Asriel against the Authority.

Just before this happens, Will, who is now in the vicinity with Lyra, takes a walk while everyone else sleeps. He is attacked in the dark by a man who turns out to be his father, but Will doesn't yet know it. They talk together and Parry tells him that another war is coming as in the past, but this time the right side must win. The world needs a fresh start and the key to victory is the subtle knife. This weapon alone can defeat the tyrant, God. Parry tells Will that the war has always been between those who want to know more and be wiser and stronger, and those who want to obey and be humble and submit. So he instructs Will to go to Lord Asriel and give him the weapon. Then, using his shaman skills, he treats Will's wound with blood moss. All seems fine until an arrow flies from the sky and kills Parry. Horrified, Will seizes the witch and discovers that she was slighted by Parry because he wished to remain faithful to his wife and this is the reason for killing his father. The witch then commits suicide!

In *His Dark Materials*, shamanism is a good thing, while church priesthood is a bad thing. Yet shamanism is just a fancy name for another priesthood. Shamans use rituals; they undergo rigorous training in esoteric disciplines that clearly separate them from lesser mortals; people come to them for wisdom. They are gurus. So why criticise the priesthood of the church and not the priesthood of shamanism? We should perhaps question the need for either form of priesthood and the whole notion of hierarchies and rituals. The New Testament does precisely that because it recognises that Jesus has inaugurated a new age and a new basis for access to God.

The New Testament teaches a universal priesthood of all true believers because they are all members of the new High Priest, Jesus, rather than just an elite corps drawn from the masses. The book of Hebrews calls this the order of Melchisedek and it is a superior replacement for the Old Testament select priesthood concept (Hebrews 7). Jesus is now the one mediator between God and man (1 Timothy 2:5), and the simplest believer can pray to the Father in his name and by the power of the Holy Spirit and guarantee to be heard.[5]

This makes authentic Christianity ultimately a religionless religion. This doesn't dismiss the place of leadership, but it's a functional role, not a magical one. Nor does it deny the power of symbolism and mysticism to help people find God, but access to the Father does not depend for its efficacy upon ceremonies, rituals or specialised priesthoods. Indeed, we look in vain for fixed rituals administered by hierarchies.

The idea of priesthood has its source in the human desire to control access to power and privilege, because the divine being or force is deemed so dangerous as to need the skills of a specially trained caste. Shamanist priesthoods put the focus on the Gnostic search for God through higher levels of initiation and often painful empathetic mediation for others. At the heart of the Christian gospel is the 'new and living way' opened by Christ when he died (Hebrews 10:20), making it possible for anyone to come to God and find acceptance in his sight. People already sanctified through the blood of Christ need no further sacrifices or offerings. Rituals will make no difference; no magic words, no special formulas will appease God, because he has already restored friendship with his creation through the death of his Son.

---

[5] Peter describes all God's people as a chosen people and a royal priesthood (1 Peter 2:9).

6

O Happy Sin!

Sometimes likened to Kafka, Heinrich von Kleist (1777–1811) was
an eighteenth-century philosopher who committed suicide at the age
of 34. He did, however, write a little essay entitled *On the Marionette
Theatre*, which Philip Pullman acknowledges to have fascinated him
and the influence of which can be seen in *His Dark Materials*.

Von Kleist uses the analogy of puppets to illustrate the grace of
unconscious movement, as opposed to the affectation of self-
conscious movement more commonly associated with adults. It's all
to do with the centre of gravity: von Kleist argues that true grace
springs from a lack of self-consciousness and even a lack of conscious
thought. Only then do we move from the soul's centre of gravity.
However, the moment we develop consciousness we're tempted to
move from other centres of gravity and our steps become jerky,
awkward and affected. In his view only puppets and animals possess
this natural virtue. To illustrate his point he describes a bear parrying a
trained sword fencer. The bear cannot be fooled because, possessing
natural grace, it is not subject to deceit. This observation is used by
Pullman in his depiction of the armoured bear, Iorek Byrnison.

Von Kleist was struggling with Kant's dictum about the ultimate
unknowability of truth; that is, our human condition by definition

limits our perception of reality so that we can only know in part. Realising himself to be a distinct entity and so separate from his surroundings, von Kleist understood that this separation prevented true knowledge. For that to be possible we would need to be indivisible from our environment, totally and unselfconsciously connected. As it is, whatever we do know must be shot through with uncertainty and doubt. We cannot ever know for sure.

Genesis rewritten

In von Kleist's view the origin and solution to this dilemma lies in Genesis 3. Not that he views it as an historical event; rather, the biblical story is for him a metaphor. It is a mythical representation of our discovery of self-awareness, and therefore of separation, and this process is repeated in the life of every human being. 'Misconceptions like this are unavoidable now that we've eaten of the tree of knowledge. But Paradise is locked and bolted, and the cherubim stands behind us. We have to go on and make the journey round the world to see if it is perhaps open somewhere at the back.'[1]

There is no way back, but there might be a way forward. We cannot undo the Fall by a return to the state of innocence – that is, we cannot become unconscious of ourselves once consciousness has occurred – but we might go forward to infinite consciousness and become as gods.

In *His Dark Materials* the possibility of full consciousness is being lost because Dust is leaking out of the universe. Someone has to stop that happening and it comes about by means of a second Fall – a redemptive re-enactment of the first Fall, which will lift us into a state of grace, not through a loss of consciousness, but by somehow gaining it in infinite measure. This is precisely where von Kleist finishes his essay. He suggests that 'we must eat again of the tree of knowledge in order to return to the state of innocence ...' and '... that's the final chapter in the history of the world'.

---

[1] Heinrich von Kleist, *On the Marionette Theatre*, 1810 (transl. Idris Parry).

We find an echo of this in Teilhard de Chardin's Omega Point, where the evolutionary destiny of the human race and of the entire cosmos meets in Christ, except that von Kleist had no place for Christ. Nor apparently does Pullman. The conflict in *His Dark Materials* is between a church that wants to prevent people from going through their personal fall from innocence into experience, and everybody else who sees this as a necessary process if ever we are to attain infinite consciousness and, to use von Kleist's term, grace by the back door. To make matters worse, the manic church with its quantum bomb has created a gaping abyss into which Dust is pouring away to goodness knows where, and with it the possibilities of us ever attaining grace. So Will and Lyra must fulfil their destiny to prevent this from happening and at the same time Lord Asriel must destroy God so that the human race is then freed to pursue its path to grace by building the republic of heaven.

The Magisterium in Geneva has decided for no good reason that Dust is the physical evidence for original sin. To give some credibility to this outlandish notion, Pullman rewrites the text of Genesis 3 in such a way as to suggest that Adam and Eve, in their innocence, were as children and thus their daemons could take any form they wanted. But once they ate the forbidden fruit, their daemons became fixed. Having been at one with their environment, they now experienced separation, and so sin, shame and death entered the world.

We may demur at a writer abusing a sacred text, without acknowledging the fact, to give apparent credibility to his personal philosophy, and wonder how, say, such an abuse of the Qu'ran would be viewed. Many will find it offensive and intellectually dishonest.[2]

---

[2] The passage in question actually reads: 'The woman said to the serpent, "We may eat fruit from the trees in the garden, but God did say, 'You must not eat fruit from the tree that is in the middle of the garden, and you must not touch it, or you will die.' " "You will not surely die," the serpent said to the woman. "For God knows that when you eat of it your eyes will be opened, and you will be like God, knowing good and evil." When the woman saw that the fruit of the tree was good for food and pleasing to the eye, and also desirable for gaining wisdom, she took some and ate it. She also gave some to her husband, who was with her, and he ate it. Then the eyes of both of them were opened, and they realised that they were naked; so they sewed fig leaves together and made coverings for themselves' (Genesis 3:2–7).

Be that as it may Pullman, following von Kleist, believes that the Garden of Eden is the key metaphor for the human condition. Just as the square root of minus one has no actual existence (at least not in this author's mathematics) but serves a necessary function to make the equations work, so Genesis 3 may not be literal but it is a necessary story to enable us to make sense of the human story. So Pullman proposes that original sin is good, because it represents the turning point in human evolution, the point when we attained consciousness; that is, we evolved from innocence to experience. For him, disobedience is a necessary part of growing up. Incidentally, the name Dust comes from an interpretation of 'for dust thou art and unto dust thou shalt return' that rewrites the text as 'thou shalt be subject to Dust'.

The notion that the Fall was a good thing is not altogether new, though it has a quite different meaning to the one Pullman puts on it. Until the 1960s the Roman Catholic church celebrated mass on Easter Saturday with the term *O felix culpa,* which begins the sentence, 'O happy sin which received as its reward so great and good a redeemer!' Nor is the idea of a blessed sin restricted to the Roman Catholics. The Protestant hymn-writer, Isaac Watts, reflects the same thought in his well-known hymn 'Jesus shall reign where'er the sun'. He has the lines:

> In him the tribes of Adam boast
> More blessings than their Father lost.

In other words, things have turned out even better than they might otherwise have done, and all's well that ends well.

The sentiment is this: if Adam and Eve hadn't sinned, then Christ's coming into the world would have been unnecessary and people would have missed the wonder of it all. The parable of the unforgiving servant suggests that those who are most aware of the corruption of their lives are the most grateful when that corruption is removed. Yet surely the thought needs heavily qualifying. The fall of Adam and Eve has hardly brought happiness to the world but rather 'death ... and all our woe'.[3] The sad fact of human history is that we appear to have learned virtually nothing for all the centuries of our life on earth. We still fight and wage war; still murder and steal and lie and cheat; still commit adultery and rape; still abuse children. Not much sign of happiness there.

The idea of Eve's sin having a good outcome and so being part of God's overall good plan provides a source of endless theological speculation between the supralapsarian and infralapsarian schools of thought. Put simply, did God put the Fall into the scheme of things as part of his original decree, arguably making him the author of sin, or was the Fall not part of the plan, implying that God was caught out, and so not really sovereign after all? It is a problem for those who view theology through a Western Enlightenment mindset, but not one that affects those of us who approach it differently.

John Milton expresses the 'happy sin' concept thus in *Paradise Lost* when he writes:

> O goodness infinite, goodness immense!
> That all this good of evil shall produce,
> And evil turn to good; more wonderful
> Than that by which creation first brought forth
> Light out of darkness![4]

Later on, William Blake, lacking a Christian doctrine of grace, was to give this a Gnostic twist and see the Fall as the happy discovery of consciousness, as Adam and Eve journey from innocence to experience. He also believed that the fortunate Fall was hijacked by the church with dire consequences for the human race. In his poem, *The Garden of Love* (1794), he writes:

> I went to the Garden of Love
> And saw what I never had seen:
> A Chapel was built in the midst,
> Where I used to play on the green.

---

[3] Quoted from the opening words of *Paradise Lost* by John Milton.
[4] Book XII.

And the gates of this Chapel were shut,
And 'Thou shalt not' writ over the door,
So I turned to the Garden of Love
That so many sweet flowers bore;

And I saw it was filled with graves,
And tombstones where flowers should be;
And Priests in black gowns were walking their rounds,
And binding with briars my joys and desires.

Philip Pullman has obviously culled his ideas from William Blake and, as with Blake, finds the church the great enemy of this so-called original sin, because the church's vested interests lie in keeping people in a state of innocence; that is, ignorance. Provided people think they are evil, then the priests can continue doling out penances, absolutions and masses, while holding out escape from hell and the promise of heaven for those who keep their rules. Pullman makes the promise completely vacuous, of course, as when the martyr cries bitterly, 'because the land of the dead isn't a place of reward or a place of punishment. It's a place of nothing.'[5]

Such is the power of the church and the pseudo-God, Authority, behind it that the only answer is to wage heroic war on both, while at the same time a new Fall, another *felix culpa*, must take place to reverse the loss of consciousness and enable us to continue forward on our evolutionary journey.

This brings us to the role of Mary Malone. Malone reaches Cittagazze and though it's not at all clear why, she seems to have the power to repel the Spectres. Knowing she must play the part of the serpent, because Dust has told her to, she consults *The Book of Changes* and uses I Ching to divine her path. She finds a window into another world, where she meets the strange animals on wheels called Mulefa. Dust, this consciousness that is draining away, has got her to the place where she can save it.

This is a redemptive offer for her. Having rejected her Christian faith in favour of a failed human love, she needs to find a point to

---

[5] *TAS*, 336.

her life. Evidently she misses God and the warmth and security that he brings. So by talking about her early experiences of sexual love and her awakening to adult sexual consciousness, she triggers the same desire in Will and Lyra, both of whom are conveniently just on the point of puberty. They begin to view each other differently; having become friends they now start to feel pubescent love for one another. Mary Malone herself has by now worked out that Dust is pouring out of the universe and, although not fully understanding what she is doing in tempting Will and Lyra, knows that something will happen that might save the world as a consequence of her involvement with them.

Sexual salvation

Since Pullman associates original sin with sex, the new Fall when it takes place is of a sexual nature. The now pubescent Lyra and Will remove their clothes in each other's presence and do so with a sense of self-awareness that was absent when they were children. They then entwine, embrace and engage in passionate kissing in a grotto. Whether they engage in full intercourse is judiciously not stated; maybe it is implicit rather than explicit. Either way, this sexual encounter is enough to make the earth move; the flow of Dust is reversed!

It is a thoroughly sacramental act, a first (and in this case last) communion which demonstrates that even 'the devil's party' cannot altogether escape Love. Pullman's wistful moment is, as Andrew Greeley puts it while reminiscing in prayer on the 'summer' films of Ingmar Bergman, 'because he is an unconscious sacramentalist who rejects the God You are and does not know that You are the Love which he celebrates, the Love which is always vulnerable, since vulnerability is the price of love'.[6] Substituting love for Love is surely an unnecessary folly when Love is the source, the inspiration and the nourisher of all our true loves.

---

[6] Andrew Greeley, *Year of Grace* (The Mercia Press, 1990).

Of course it is by now too late for the God of *His Dark Materials* to stop Will and Lyra because he has blown away as so much dust in the wind, but there is still the church to reckon with. Earlier in the plot, a witch overhears Mrs Coulter seducing Sir Charles Coltrom into revealing that Will has the subtle knife of Cittagazze, also known as teleutaia makhaira, a last knife, or Aesahaettr. Mrs Coulter poisons Sir Charles and then captures the witch by letting a Spectre seize her daemon. The witch confesses to Mrs Coulter Lyra's real purpose: 'her new name is Eve, Mother of All, Eve again, Mother Eve'.[7] Mrs Coulter releases the Spectres from earthboundness to attack the witches in the sky for reasons that appear to be entirely nasty, but she now knows she must destroy Lyra to prevent another Fall. She realises too that Asriel will make war on the Authority, as in the first heavenly war, but this time she is determined to prevent Eve from falling.

Mrs Coulter is an enigmatic personality, and out of a supposed love for her daughter, she somewhat implausibly changes her mind later on. She and Lord Asriel finally drag the Metatron into the abyss in an act of heroic self-sacrifice, allowing Lyra to continue on her destined path. Undaunted, however, the church continues the pursuit. The children must be caught and Dust must be destroyed, even if that means destroying everybody else. Better no world than a world of sin, they decree. So the church makes plans to kill Lyra and it grants pre-emptive penance and absolution to one Father Gomez, so that he can commit the sin of murder without conscience. Gomez is told to look not for the child, but for the tempter of the child – a woman from another world. In other words, Mary Malone.

Gomez reaches the world of the Mulefa and, armed with a rifle, arrives on the scene just as Will and Lyra are locked in the passionate embrace of their first sexual love. But before he can do anything, the angel Balthamos appears, seizes Gomez's daemon and succeeds in killing the priest. The plot has failed. Mary

---

7 *TSK*, 328.

Malone sees the children returning hand in hand and they are covered in Dust that is now pouring from the sky. Both she and the Mulefa note that the flow of Dust from the universe has ceased. The children's sexual awakening has saved the world!

In real life it isn't as simple as that, of course. Indeed, underage sexual activity among children appears to be doing anything but save the world. Given the disastrous state of affairs among Western societies, with their soaring teenage pregnancies, abortions, sexually transmitted diseases, broken homes, single-parent families, confused identities and the like, it hardly suggests that this is the path to redemption.

The notion of sexual salvation was popularised in the 1960s, the idea being that if people could have the freedom to indulge their sexual desires at will, then society would be so much healthier, there would be less stress, fewer neuroses and hardly any need for medication and counselling at all. Whatever the benefits of loosening up some of the sexual mores of mid-twentieth-century society, and there were some, we may express more than a little scepticism at the supposed transformation said to be wrought by such wholesale permissiveness.

The idea that sex is what the Fall was all about is popular but erroneous, and leads to the mistaken conclusion that the church which doesn't like sin also doesn't like sex. Yet even a cursory reading of the Genesis account makes it clear that Adam and Eve were not created as children; whatever their 'innocence' was it was certainly not sexual innocence. Created as adults, God had already granted to them the gift of sexual love and oneness: 'So God created man in his own image, in the image of God he created him; male and female he created them. God blessed them and said to them, "Be fruitful and increase in number" ' (Genesis 1:27–28). The second chapter records: 'The man said, "This is now bone of my bones and flesh of my flesh; she shall be called 'woman', for she was taken out of man." For this reason a man will leave his father and mother and be united to his wife, and they will become one flesh. The man and his wife were both naked, and they felt no shame' (Genesis 2:23–25). Even those who deny the historicity of this record and treat it as a metaphor will be obliged to find a different interpretation to that imposed on it in *His Dark Materials* if they are to have any regard for the plain meaning of the text.

It would be foolish and dishonest to deny that there have been some elements of the church that have held for periods of time an anti-pleasure and anti-sex philosophy. However, we must maintain that those who take such a position are denying the very scriptures they claim to believe. Paul, in a letter to Timothy, warns:

> The Spirit clearly says that in later times some will abandon the faith and follow deceiving spirits and things taught by demons. Such teachings come through hypocritical liars, whose consciences have been seared as with a hot iron. They forbid people to marry and order them to abstain from certain foods, which God created to be received with thanksgiving by those who believe and who know the truth. For everything God created is good, and nothing is to be rejected if it is received with thanksgiving. (1 Timothy 4:1–4)

This is consistent with the New Testament insistence that there is no intrinsic merit in asceticism or sexual abstinence. So, as we noted earlier, Paul writes to the Corinthians:

> Since there is so much immorality, each man should have his own wife, and each woman her own husband. The husband should fulfil his marital duty to his wife, and likewise the wife to her husband. The wife's body does not belong to her alone but also to her husband. In the same way, the husband's body does not belong to him alone but also to his wife. Do not deprive each other except by mutual consent and for a time, so that you may devote yourselves to prayer. Then come together again. (1 Corinthians 7:2–5)

In short the Bible is strongly in favour of sex and marriage as a good and pleasurable gift from God. What it opposes is promiscuity, and that because of its destructive effects upon the human race. It has nothing to do with the church wanting to control procreation or pleasure. It's simply because that's how the Maker best intended things to work.

Original goodness

Pullman's view of a happy sexual Fall, a redefined 'original sin', may suit those who live in an immensely privileged and protected Western middle-class world – they can afford to dance with the daisies in some sort of pantheistic dreamland – but the rest of the human race has to face the realities of human nature and try to do something about the immense suffering of a fallen world. Nor will it do to suggest that all this evil is because of the controlling influence of either God or the church. Human nature is inherently corrupt, whether we like it or not, and no amount of sophistry will avoid that stark fact. Getting rid of God and the church would hardly seem to suffice: to judge by the great atheistic experiments conducted on millions of people during the twentieth century, it does anything but solve the problems.

We must return to our interpretation of Genesis 3. The story should be read at face value. Genesis answers a number of simple questions asked by children and adults alike: How did we get here? Why do we wear clothes? Why are people nasty? Why is God difficult to know? Why do we die? Why are there weeds? Why is work hard? Why do Mummy and Daddy have rows?

To answer these questions, and contrary to the church's emphasis in *His Dark Materials*, Genesis begins not with original sin but with original goodness. Adam and Eve were created in the image of God and had an incredible potential for goodness. In the words of Psalm 8: 'What is man that you are mindful of him, the son of man that you care for him? You made him a little lower than the heavenly beings and crowned him with glory and honour. You made him ruler over the works of your hands; you put everything under his feet' (Psalm 8:4–6).

To be truly in the image of God, God had to grant Adam and Eve genuine freedom. They had the ability to make choices, and that provided a role for a tempter. Leaving aside unanswerable questions about how the tempter ever became a tempter, Adam and Eve fell for the lie. They submitted to the only three possible temptations: what the apostle John calls 'the lust of the flesh, and the lust of the eyes, and the pride of life' (1 John 2:16, AV). Self-gratification, covetousness and pride. As a result, instead of learning to live their lives in harmony with their Creator and evolving into an infinity of grace and truth, they began to learn the hard way. Their spiritual genes mutated and they passed this on to their descendants, giving what we now take to be the human condition: environmental alienation, difficulties with sex and childbirth, marital strife, self-consciousness and, worst of all, physical and spiritual death. In truth, the first sin led to dust, not to Dust. It resulted in a loss of consciousness, a loss of life. So Paul writes, '... in Adam all die' (1 Corinthians 15:22).

However, we must not leave it there. Paul continues, 'In Christ all will be made alive.' The soured soil of Genesis 3 contains the seed of hope. One day the woman will have a descendant who will bring about the salvation of the human race. Not by an inverted repeat of the Fall, but by the sacrificial offering of himself. The passion of Christ saves us, not the passion of sex.

The doctrine of Darwinism that undergirds *His Dark Materials* finds the above unacceptable, of course. Pullman himself has stated that in spite of his childhood belief in the Christian faith, when he reached adulthood, he could no longer reconcile Darwinism and the Bible, and felt that the Bible had to go. That may be a questionable choice to have made in the light of the inherent scientific weaknesses of Darwinism and of the evils that it has spawned, but it is a common one.[8] Once adopt that position and there remains little choice but to turn the Genesis story into some metaphor for growing up, and not necessarily even to do that with an accurate regard for the text.

In *His Dark Materials* the church is presented as holding a pathologically negative view of human nature based upon its

---

[8] A good scientific and philosophic case can be made for creationism, but political correctness excludes it from significant airing. If the intellectual censorship and bigotry were removed and creationism were able to be presented with similar resources to those used by Darwinists, it might make an equal if not much more persuasive case for the origin of things.

doctrine of original sin. Clearly the church in *HDM* is prepared to go to extreme lengths to prevent original sin, let alone its recurrence, yet presumably finds it a useful doctrine for keeping people under control. It's a distasteful notion and one by and large rejected by Western society when it comes to the nature–nurture debate. Are we born bad, or are we made bad? Current educational theory is unequivocal. Teachers are trained to believe in the potential of every child rather than in the need for every child to be corrected. They no longer even have trial and error; nowadays it's trial and improvement. As the L'Oreal advert has it, 'Because I'm worth it!'[9]

Muslims too argue that Islam believes in original goodness and the capability of human beings to grow from a positive self-image into obedience to Allah. This appears to contrast starkly with those who talk of the total depravity of the human race. Or original sin. The doctrine of original sin is not stated as such in the Scriptures but was formulated by the church under the influence of Augustine. Yet even here it seems to have meant not so much a case of total depravity within the nature of the individual – if by that we mean they are incapable of any act of goodness, as some extreme Calvinists would have it – as to do with being in Adam.

This is the biblical concept of federal headship: people bear the consequences of Adam's action just as, say, a nation bears the consequences if its leader decides to go to war. Suddenly the whole nation is at war. Positively, Christ is the second man, the last Adam, as Paul describes him in 1 Corinthians 15, who comes to give life. So people who put their faith in Christ move from being in Adam to being in Christ. They leave behind the old

---

[9] Without doubt children should be given an environment of encouragement rather than be told how useless they are, let alone be punished for their failure to achieve what they sincerely tried to achieve. But it's only half the story, failing to recognise as it does the inherent selfishness in human nature that no amount of mere education takes away. Indeed, the Darwinist philosophy positively encourages selfishness, with its ideology of the survival of the fittest and fastest. The Bible faces the egotistical side of human nature square on, but it does not do so at the expense of the need to encourage children in their self-worth.

man (Adam) and become part of the corporate new man (Christ). And that is truly how we get rid of what some have dubbed original sin.

The Fall cut human beings off from fellowship with God and brought all manner of evil upon the world, but it did not corrupt us completely. There remains the spark of divine life because we are still made in the image of God. So it is marred goodness rather than total depravity. And the Bible makes it clear that people are capable of genuinely good sacrificial acts. That is the point of Romans 2, where Paul says that God will 'give to each person according to what he has done. To those who by persistence in doing good seek glory, honour and immortality, he will give eternal life' (Romans 2:7). In other words, it's possible for people to do good, just as it's possible for us to do evil. Whatever else Adam and Eve did, they certainly did not make the human race utterly corrupt beyond redemption. People still have consciences that are God-given, and there is a clear restraint on human evil that we ourselves desire. If we were utterly corrupt we would make no laws to restrain evil and no one would believe in the benefits of good behaviour. Nor would we be able to distinguish between the sins that we all commit and those acts of barbaric evil like torture, genocide and slavery.

Christians who lack a doctrine of common grace will struggle with this. One of my own novels was criticised in America because the two central characters, a man and a woman, lived together outside of wedlock, but evidently loved one another. It was suggested that their love must have been a sham because fallen creatures aren't capable of altruism. The book was criticised because it didn't make that ludicrous point. Perhaps it's this version of the doctrine of original sin that so incenses people like Philip Pullman – and I will sympathise!

The Roman Catholic catechism teaches that infant baptism has the specific technical purpose of removing the stain of original sin. It does not solve all the problems; Catholic theology still teaches the need for a process of conversion. For them, infant baptism places a person, in terms of their status, into Christ and his body, but it is still necessary in their formulation for the person to deal with that innate selfishness of human nature that we call sin.

Most Protestants would see it differently, and the evangelicals would believe that it comes about by means of a conscious confession of faith in Christ rather than the application of holy water to a baby's head, however sincere the promises of those present. Many denominations reserve those promises for the candidate's adult baptism. In spite of these differences the technical point still stands. If original sin is conceived of in federal terms, then regeneration deals with it. To believe in original sin in this sense is not the same as saying we believe in total depravity in the sense of there being nothing good about human nature.

At the same time we humans are sinners: our nature is corrupted by the Fall and we are in need of salvation. That salvation, as we shall see later, cannot come about by our own efforts. We need help because we are still trapped in that part of the human race known as 'in Adam'. The good news is that help is at hand. In the words of John Newman's hymn, 'A second Adam to the fight, and to the rescue came', and his name is Jesus.

The underlying idea in *His Dark Materials* is that the human race needs a fresh start. We can dismiss as frivolous the notion that a quasi-sexual act by two pubescent children could bring this about, but we should give attention to God's universal invitation for people to enter a redeemed race with a fresh start in Christ: 'If anyone is in Christ, he is a new creation; the old has gone, the new has come!' (2 Corinthians 5:17). That promise of personal renewal is the harbinger of a totally renewed cosmos, where all things are reconciled and where our Christ capacity will come to its full flowering. To return for a moment to Kant and to von Kleist, the apostle Paul might agree that we 'know in part', but he is able to look to the future in the love of God and declare, '... then I shall know fully, even as I am fully known' (1 Corinthians 13:12).

This knowledge, this total connectivity, comes about not by eating again of the tree of the knowledge of good and evil but by regaining through Christ access to the fruit of other trees in the garden – the tree of life, no less![10]

---

[10] Genesis 2:8–9.

7

Those Evil Christians!

AN AUTHOR'S PREJUDICES AND THE STATE OF THE CHURCH

Philip Pullman was born in Norwich in 1946 and was educated at Ysgol Ardudwy in Harlech, Wales. His father was an RAF officer, who died during the Mau Mau uprisings in Kenya when Pullman was seven years of age. He and his brother went to live with his mother's parents until his mother remarried. With his stepfather, the family moved to Australia and then back to Wales.

He studied English at Exeter College, Oxford, and graduated in 1968. After a number of jobs he returned to Oxford in 1973 to teach in various middle schools, and in 1986 he became a part-time senior lecturer on the Victorian novel and the folk tale at Westminster College, Oxford. He quit this job in 1996 to write full-time and he has had a number of books published, for both adults and children, quite apart from *His Dark Materials*.

We may wonder why he should be so against the church and against God. To spend seven years of one's life producing a work in which this is a significant theme suggests more than a passing dislike, and we might suspect that someone must have rattled his cage along the way for him to have developed such an antipathy. But if so, he is being very coy about it. In fact, he describes his upbringing as conventionally middle class, complete with Sunday school and church attendance, choir and confirmation. His grand-father was a clergyman and by all accounts a very kind man who showed much love and care for Pullman and his brother.

There is no hint of paedophile priests, or choirmasters running off with the church secretary. No painful rejection by a woman. Pullman has been married since 1970, he has two adult sons and there is no suggestion of scandal about any of them. As we noted earlier, if we want to find reasons for his personal antipathy to the Christian faith, we will have to look at an adolescent loss of childhood faith in favour of Darwinian evolutionism, which he found to be a more intellectually convincing version of human origins.

Bigotry

Yet his mentors have instilled a deeper bigotry. When he describes his anger at the church he says it's because of

> the record of the Inquisition, persecuting heretics and torturing Jews and all that sort of stuff; and it comes from the other side, too, from the Protestants burning the Catholics. It comes from the insensate pursuit of innocent and crazy old women, and from the Puritans in America burning and hanging witches – and it comes not only from the Christian church but also the Taliban. Every single religion that has a monotheistic god ends up by persecuting other people.[1]

This is, of course, a challenging statement. However, persecution has never been the sole province of monotheistic cultures. Polytheists such as Hindus also persecute other people, as do tribal animists, as do atheists and agnostics. What would Pullman say about the atheistic North Korean policy of imprisoning and torturing children for having the wrong kind of parents, for example? Oppression is a human condition, not a religious one. But perhaps such immoderate statements spring from disappoint-ment rather than hatred. Pullman wants to cover his odds on the

---

[1] 'Heat and Dust', interview with Huw Spanner, *Third Way*, April 2002.

atheist–agnostic question on the grounds that he has insufficient evidence to make a final decision – which would leave him agnostic – but within the evidence of his own experience he is a convinced atheist. Nonetheless he retains a respect for Unitarians and Quakers because they tolerate differences of opinion, and he also acknowledges that Jesus was a moral genius who had a great deal of good to say. Moreover, he concedes that the kingdom of heaven promised 'happiness and a sense of purpose ... a place in the universe ... a role and a destiny that were noble and splendid'.[2]

For all that, the King is dead, or at least the parody that Pullman paints is, and although Pullman still needs the things that heaven promised, he is convinced that now he must bring them about on earth in a republic.

Pullman claims that he is not making an argument or preaching a sermon, or setting out a political tract. He is simply telling the story and considers himself the servant of the story, enjoying the technical business of putting it together, earning a living and making some sense of his experience of the world. That's fair enough as far as it goes – and he is a good storyteller – but it is stretching our credulity to say that's all it is. Likewise, in the same interview quoted above, when asked why he portrayed all his Christian characters as uniformly bad, Pullman put it down to an artistic flaw on his part. But it isn't; Pullman is too talented for that. This has all the marks of a polemical work, not least in its caricaturing of the opponents as having no redeeming features whatsoever. And it is cunningly done. He has created a world so near to our own, so interwoven, and portrayed the church in such sweeping terms that it would be difficult not to believe that the church is much different in our own age or any other.

This polemical element does weaken *His Dark Materials*. Arguably it could have been a better story without the anti-church stuff, for in setting up a straw man in his attack on the church Pullman has created characters that are so utterly one dimensional

---

[2] *Ibid.*

that he falls into the very fault of those whom he is criticising. It is, after all, a defining characteristic of fundamentalist bigots to make wholesale and damning accusations against those they disagree with and to present them in the most distastefully irredeemable terms. In Pullman's portrayal of the church we find nothing but clichéd stereotypical caricatures – all the old chestnuts: witch-hunting, torture, paedophilia, political expediency, moral casuistry, fanatical devotion, and not a real character in sight. It's cowboys and Indians, with the church cast in the role of the Indians the way it was in Hollywood films when Indians were just the enemy, with no regard for their lives, character or culture. This is a shame because his descriptive writing is brilliant and his artist's eye for detail and mood enables us to visualise and experience his scenes with wonderful vividness.

Without wishing to venture too far into the realms of literary criticism, nonetheless we could wish for more character development in some of the main players. Lord Asriel comes across as no more than a bombastic Victorian music hall character – all melodramatic theatricality and little depth. Mrs Coulter pops in and out of the story like some kind of manipulative and sadistic arch devil, but we never get to know what makes her tick on the inside. Her origins are unknown; all we have from Lord Asriel by way of explanation for her behaviour is that she is power hungry, having first sought to get power through marriage and then later through the church.

Even her change of heart fails fully to convince. *The Amber Spyglass* opens with her keeping her daughter in a drugged sleep in a Himalayan cave. Later on, when Lord Asriel has captured her and she is tied to a chair in his chamber, she confesses to having had an unanticipated change of heart regarding her daughter. But we never get inside her heart to find out why. All she can say is that she is now an enemy of the church and is prepared to side with Asriel against the Authority to protect her daughter while she plays the necessary role of Eve. She knows the church will kill Lyra rather than let this happen because Calvin ordered the deaths of children. She is also shocked to learn that the Authority did not create everything, but was a rebel angel.

In this interview Lord Asriel tells her that he wants to build his republic without kings, bishops or priests, and he takes her to see a machine called the intention craft – a remarkable contraption that is guided by the intentions of the pilot. She hijacks the craft and escapes, but clever Asriel has anticipated this. He has a better machine hidden away and knows that Mrs Coulter will now spy for him. But we still don't know what really motivates her.

Of the other key characters, Mary Malone is a dislocated and distracted figure, but we get nearer to her inner workings than those of any other, especially when she describes her confused journey and her inner contradictions. She is perhaps the most sympathetically drawn character in the trilogy and her description of how she discovered romantic love has an authentic ring to it. Meanwhile, Will and Lyra are children, so we must allow for their characters to be in development. The overriding characteristic of both is a focused determination to do what they believe to be right, a childish sense of justice that carries them stoically through their adventures. However, there is little development of their relationship in preparation for their eventual sexual encounter.

These are weaknesses in the storytelling and are allowable. Yet should we object to Pullman's cynical caricature of the church? Some fans of his work have already decided that anyone who objects must be a raving fundamentalist, but that is just a facile smear word too easily applied and reflects only the prejudices of those who do so.

The grounds for any objection must be based on misrepresentation. Is the church in our world anything like the one portrayed in Lyra's world? Our perception is that Pullman wants us to draw some comparisons, and negative ones at that, but is he justified in doing so? Is the church in reality a monolithic sinister organisation bent on destroying happiness in the name of a legalistic religion? If not, then all we are looking at is an extended instance of the old-fashioned intolerance reminiscent of the early 1960s 'death of

God' nonsense and the belligerent atheism of those days. It all seems very dated in a postmodern generation that has more respect for the beliefs of others than that cantankerous old humanism ever did.

The church that Pullman portrays is neither altogether medieval nor modern. It is Roman Catholic, but as we noted earlier its last pope was John Calvin and the church is now based at Geneva, not Rome. This is Pullman's way of lumping together what he sees as both types of Christian fundamentalism and ecclesiastical authority.

We must be careful not to defend the indefensible. Calvin's attitude towards those who differed from him, for example, was quite as bigoted as that of his earlier Catholic opponents. Nor shall we attempt to justify the Inquisition or those situations where Machiavellian politics combines with the interests of the church to create a monster. Much of what Pullman accuses the church of has occurred at some times and in some parts of the church's long international history. Our problem is with the sweeping statements that suggest all of the church is like this all of the time.

Portraying the church as incorrigibly evil and filled with sadists, paedophiles, fanatical lunatics and other deviants reveals an author's bigotry. The fact that a few have behaved in such a manner and so contrary to the teachings of Christ hardly justifies writing off the whole institution. Following such logic, we would encourage children to avoid schools because of the number of paedophile teachers and ancillary staff within the ranks of the profession. And nobody would go to a general practitioner for fear that they might be poisoned to death by another Dr Harold Shipman. On such ludicrous parameters we would have to demonise the entire teaching profession and the entire medical profession. And people who do that are generally encouraged to seek help.

Individuals are fallible and it is beyond the ability of any human organisation, even with divine blessing, to prevent either infiltration or the corruption of a minority of its members and leaders. Nobody wants to minimise the problems raised by such failings;

indeed, in the case of the church they are more of a problem for those within than for those outside. Few in their right minds would ever claim that the church is infallible. Yet nor is any other institution; hypocrisy is a problem common to humanity and it will hardly do to witch-hunt the church when all human institutions are shot through with corruption – and often to a far greater extent than the church even in its most decadent moments has ever sunk.

We may ask why Pullman has chosen a soft target like the church, rather than taking on the corruption in, say, Islam. Perhaps he knows that the church is anything but like the way it's portrayed in *His Dark Materials*. To the best of my knowledge, Christians do not issue fatwahs against authors and he will have no need to live in hiding, in fear of his life because of persecution by the church.

That said, it hasn't always been the case, and however much we say that the church has learned from its unsavoury episodes in the past, we must sympathise with Pullman's concerns. Given certain conditions the danger is never far away. Witness those fundamentalists in America who have resorted to violence to advance the cause of Christ. Of course, that is not a mainstream orthodox position, and most Christians are aghast and appalled by their actions and would in no way wish to associate themselves with such people. The vast majority of the many millions of Christian believers around the world are good, peace-loving people who totally reject those fundamentalist extremes and recognise that those who use physical violence and crude censorship to further their cause do not have the spirit of Christ, the Prince of Peace. Indeed, biblical Christians have actually over the centuries fought for the freedom of expression and faith, and still do so throughout the world today.

However, we need to look a little deeper at this issue. It is all very well to say that the world is worse than the church, to point out that violence and repression are not the sole province of monotheistic faiths, but that still doesn't deal with why Christians of all people should lapse into these errors. We can't even say that biblical Christians are always peacemakers; some of the worst have been deep students of the Bible and expert theologians. Calvin was one such, but he still wrote, 'Whoever shall now contend that it is unjust to put heretics and blasphemers to death will knowingly and willingly incur their very guilt.' It surely betrays the very mindset of intolerant zeal that Pullman attacks.

Sacralism

The problem arises because of sacralism. Leonard Verduin defined this as the unholy fusion of the church and the state.[3] It's not a problem unique to Christianity. State religions have existed from at least as far back as Egyptian and Babylonian times, and most often the monarch has been either God himself or God's chosen infallible representative or manifestation. It exists wherever personal belief is subject to state sanction as, for example, in modern Saudi Arabia, where Islam is the official religion both endorsed and intimately entwined with the state. It's a sacral faith. The same principle applied in Nazi Germany and in communist Russia. Witness the veneration of both Hitler and Lenin during those years, and we are confronted with a wholly religious phenomenon in a political context.

Sacralism always leads to coercion, political correctness and the censorship of free speech, and even free thought. George Orwell sounded the warning back in 1948 in his novel *Nineteen Eighty-Four*. It's a note that still needs to be sounded. Big Brother takes many guises, and fundamentalism today isn't confined to those of overtly religious persuasions. The secular intellectual establishment has its own form of totalitarian fundamentalism that increasingly tells people what they may or may not believe, sometimes enforced with criminal and social sanctions.

Sacralism is about power and control: the excessive zeal that believes a cause can be advanced and maintained only by taking

---

[3] Leonard Verduin, *The Reformers and Their Stepchildren* (Eerdmans Publishing Co., 1964).

the shortcut of coercion rather than the longer but more fruitful journey of presenting the truth and allowing individuals to respond. Beneath sacralism lies doubt, the uncertainty that what we are saying really does stand up on its own merits. The early church flourished in a situation of sacral oppression from the Roman government because it was not a sacral faith and didn't need the sword of the state to advance its cause. In fact, Jesus famously drew a clear distinction between the kingdoms of this world and the kingdom of God when he declared, 'Give to Caesar what is Caesar's, and to God what is God's' (Matthew 22:21).

The New Testament recognised the legitimacy of the state to uphold law and order and to defend its people. For that privilege it could levy taxes and people might grant the state a degree of loyalty, irrespective of their religious orientation. The role of the church wasn't to seek political power, either directly or through the mechanisms of the state; it was instead called to act as salt and light. In other words, to be a redemptive influence on the state. When a state recognises this, it benefits enormously from the Christian input, but when the state seeks to hijack the church for its own ends, the church suffers corruption. And when the state is hijacked to do the church's dirty work, as in, say, the burning of Servetus, the church has sold out on its own gospel. For the church has no right to coerce people. It can only ask loyalty of those who are by their own free choice believers in Christ, because it isn't in the nature of God to coerce those whom he loves. Ideas and beliefs may be worth dying for, but they are not worth killing for.

The gospel is actually hindered and contradicted when it gets entangled with the sword of violence or with political and economic coercion. It is, after all, the offer of God's free grace – a promise of forgiveness and a call to follow the new King of kings and Lord of lords, who laid down his life for his sheep. He's the Good Shepherd and the Prince of Peace, not the tyrant. 'To us a child is born, to us a son is given, and the government will be on his shoulders. And he will be called Wonderful Counsellor, Mighty God, Everlasting Father, Prince of Peace' (Isaiah 9:6). His name is certainly not Coercive Dictator.

Much of Western Christianity fell foul of sacralism following the conversion of Constantine in AD 313. This led to a much welcomed cessation of state persecution, but the Roman state wanted to extend its power and control, and Constantine never lost the old 'genius of Caesar' mentality. Soon, he was using the church as an instrument of imperial policy. That paradigm continued to undergird the discussions between the state and the church, and led in time to the Holy Roman Empire, another sacral state in which the lines between the state's responsibilities and the church's values would continually be blurred. In effect, in the name of Christianity, they created a pre-Christian sacral society, with all the attendant evils now done in the name of Christ. Needless to say it led to compromise and hypocrisy, and it limited the spread of the gospel to the constraints of political precepts, rather than releasing it according to the apostolic mandate to offer all mankind freely the opportunity to receive Christ as Lord and Saviour.

By no means everybody was happy with this state of affairs. Throughout history there were vast numbers of Christians who followed the biblical norms laid down by Jesus, and they were the ones often persecuted by the church state and called heretics. The Reformation, when it came in Britain, though in many ways much needed, was still a church state act under Henry VIII and it perpetuated the problems of sacralism. Leonard Verduin's book, *The Reformers and Their Stepchildren*, explores the difficult journey into freedom by those 'stepchildren' who carried the torch for a return to the teachings of Jesus and the New Testament apostles. They were the forerunners of the non-Episcopal churches of today, and perhaps their greatest legacy was the founding of the

United States of America as a place where the freedom to worship was dictated only by conscience and not by the coercive power of the state.[4]

A healthy church

Those of us who work for the radical return of the church to its non-coercive but wonderfully persuasive message of love, forgiveness, reconciliation, peace and transformation see a very different picture of the church from that presented in *His Dark Materials*. Ours is the story of the church as an almost unqualified good in a world of corruption, self-interest and political opportunism. We side with Tertullian, who was able to say in the third century, with a real measure of truth, that not only did the church care for all its own poor, but it cared for the poor in the rest of the Empire as well.[5] In effect, the church had instituted the first social services. Nor was it a flash in the pan; later on the anti-Christian pagan, Julian the Apostate, was forced to the same conclusion.[6]

This church pioneered medicine and free education for all. It originated our great centres of learning, hospitals and health services throughout the world. In the United Kingdom, the formation of the National Health Service was profoundly influenced by the nonconformist Christian conscience in the nineteenth century and the Christian socialist movement in the twentieth century. The same is true of the early trades union movement. It is a church that engages in the major hands-on famine relief programmes of the world, and does more to help the victims of HIV and AIDS, including homosexuals, than any other single

---

[4] Not that it's all rosy in the USA. The tables have rather turned and today religious freedom is under attack not from the church so much as from the liberal establishment that now seeks to persecute Christianity out of existence in the very forums where the founders of the United States believed freedom of expression was a virtue.

[5] Tertullian, *Apology*.

[6] 'These godless Galileans [i.e. Christians] feed not only their own poor but ours: our poor lack our care' (Ep. Sozom. 5:16).

institution in the world. Christians provide the biggest single
voluntary workforce in many nations. If they were to pull the plug
on their goodwill in, say, the United Kingdom, economically the
nation would be hard pressed to cope with the colossal need that
Christians quietly get on with meeting day after day and year after
year.

Nor does the church do this simply to proselytise. Love for
one's neighbour is born from a genuine altruism. It is Christians'
faith in Jesus Christ that motivates them to care and not simply the
desire to make proselytes – though it should not necessarily be
thought a bad thing if it were the latter. The gospel is good news.
Jesus said, 'I have come that they may have life, and have it to the
full' (John 10:10). The gospel transforms people's inner motiva-
tions, hopes and dreams. It lifts them from self-despair, cynicism
and arrogance to a place where once filled with the Holy Spirit of
God, they can take control of their destiny, experience the healing
of their inner angst, establish stable and loving relationships and
become a force of positive good in society. Why should anyone,
except a bigot and a hypocrite, want to oppose that?

It's no good persecuting Christians and forbidding them to
express their faith in the context of their mercy ministry when
that's the very thing that inspires the ministry in the first place.
That is plainly unjust, and a denial of their human right to practise
their religion according to their conscience – a situation that
prevails in much of the world. For the church of Jesus Christ
endures more unjust persecution than any other organisation on
earth and little is done to stop it.[7]

In setting the record straight, we have no wish to idealise the
church any more than the Bible does. Albeit bigoted, Pullman
sounds a warning note in *His Dark Materials*, and it is a warning

---

[7] It is beyond the scope of this book to comment upon the contribution of the
Christian faith to art and culture. To do justice to Christ-inspired architecture,
music, art, film, literature and drama would require a volume in itself. Suffice it to
say that this great well of creativity owes its source not to repression but to a
genuine freedom of the Spirit released through the gospel of Christ.

to be heeded – and in this he might once again be found to serve God's party rather than the devil's. The church of the future needs to be one of constant self-examination and renewal and never to rest on its laurels, and it needs to be careful never to fall into the trap that Philip Pullman so ably exposes. It must reject the trappings of power and see its contribution to society as one of provocative influence for good. The church should be a pressure group calling for moral and spiritual improvement, and it should seek to defend and advocate the cause of the weak and vulnerable in society. It should also be a church prepared to challenge the vested interests of the intellectual status quo and to unmask the hypocrisy, deception and futility of anti-theistic doctrines foisted upon the world by those who should know better.

A healthy church will be unashamed of its message. It will not simply try to be popular or to conform to the fashions of the age. After all, the merely religious will always find the gospel a stumbling-block, and the sophists of the world will continue to consider it foolishness (see 1 Corinthians 1:22–23). The message is the authentic and radical message of the age, and it is needed more than ever in a decadent, complacent Western world. By all means recast the idioms and language and illustrations and presentation styles, but let people hear the simple but compelling story of Jesus Christ. It has the power to release faith and hope and love like nothing else. The timeless tale of redemption needs no modification, watering down or compromising. 'The Son of Man came to seek and to save what was lost' (Luke 19:10). People have lost God's love and they need his redemption. It's as straightforward as that.

The real grace of Christianity lies not in its institutional power, but in its incarnational love. When a vast army of ordinary people live Christlike lives by the power of the Holy Spirit, and demonstrate not just that they are nice, but that there is a sacrificial love and infectious joy and a profound peace emanating from their lives, then people will take notice of them.

Jesus told his disciples that they were the salt of the earth and the light of the world, and said, 'Let your light shine before men, that they may see your good deeds and praise your Father in heaven' (Matthew 5:16). The name of God will be redeemed when the church ceases to be either a mechanism for power or a ghetto for the pathetic, and instead engages in the task of bringing a genuine spirituality to the normality of life – in the world, but not of it. Exactly like Jesus. And that's no parody.

8

Heaven's Awful Monarch!

In July AD 144 a ship owner from Sinope, on the Black Sea, separated himself from the Catholic church to found his own brotherhood. His name was Marcion, and his movement grew rapidly. Marcion rejected the allegorising approach to the Old Testament that had become popular in the church, and instead insisted on reading it literally. What he found offended him deeply: 'He saw a God who had created a world full of the most deplorable imperfections; a God who created men, and drove them to fall into sin; who frequently repented of what he had done, and who overlooked the most serious sins in his favourites, although he punished them cruelly in others.'[1]

What Marcion read about God in the Old Testament, he saw daily in the imperfection, cruelty and repulsiveness of life. He concluded that the Old Testament was telling the truth and that God, though not absolutely evil, was of inferior worth, unable to deliver his own plans and needing to enforce a series of commandments by a system of punishments resting upon the idea of retaliation. He became convinced that Jesus came to reject this

---

[1] Hans Leitzmann, *A History of the Early Church*, Vol. 1.

Old Testament God and to reveal a new God previously unknown, who was God the Father and full of love and compassion. He concluded that the apostle Paul and the gospel writer Luke had understood this alone of all the other apostles, yet Marcion believed that even Paul's text had been corrupted by Judaisers (those who insisted that the Christian faith remain a sect of Judaism, complete with circumcision and ceremonial law), so he set about editing the text to correct it.

Long before, Plato had proposed a being called the Demi-urge. The Demi-urge was the creator of the universe. The idea crept into Gnosticism (a form of esoteric rationalism or higher knowledge of the mysteries of the universe that later infected and threatened to destroy the early church), where the Demi-urge became a heavenly being subordinate to the Supreme Being. It wasn't difficult in due course to identify Marcion's Old Testament God with the Demi-urge.

Marcion was seeking to cope with the problem of evil. Why does God allow all the suffering? If he were good, then he would stop it, and if he can't, then he's not God. Either he's not good enough or he's not God enough.

This over-simplistic analysis is a piece of monofilament thinking and is the equivalent of saying that a table has four legs and a horse has four legs, therefore a horse must be a table. To distinguish between a horse and a table requires considerably more information, as well as a context for that information. Marcion's thinking failed to take account of all the issues relating to divine sovereignty and permission, let alone the place of human free will, the work of Satan and the fallen state of the cosmos – to name but a few.

Marcion had evidently failed to understand properly the abrogation of law through Jesus Christ and his sacrificial death. Nor had he grasped the redemptive purpose of God mediated through the children of Israel, let alone the necessity of people learning the futility of trying to work out their own salvation. So instead of seeing the Old Testament scenario as portraying the reality of what happens when freely constituted people reject the will of God, Marcion simply blamed God for everything that went wrong. He never saw that God was working a revelatory and redemptive process through human history.

The death of God

It's one thing to suggest that we have only a partial revelation of God's character in the Old Testament, but quite another to suggest that he is bad or fallible in comparison to the better one revealed by Jesus Christ. The Bible draws no such distinctions between the God of the Old Testament and the God of the New. In fact the opposite, because it presents Jesus as the perfect revelation of the God of the Old Testament as he really was: 'For the law was given through Moses; grace and truth came through Jesus Christ. No-one has ever seen God, but God the One and Only, who is at the Father's side, has made him known' (John 1:17–18). In other words, we must back-read the Old Testament through the lens of Jesus and his relationship with a loving heavenly Father if we are to grasp a true understanding of the nature of God.

The reason for bringing up the subject of Marcion and the Demi-urge is because of the similarities with the pathologically negative image of God painted by Pullman in *His Dark Materials*. The Authority, as he calls him, appears to be in character very much like the Demi-urge, a rather nasty and fallible Old Testament god – to misrepresent Milton, truly 'heaven's awful monarch'!

Pullman goes further, as we have seen. The God in *His Dark Materials* is not the Creator, nor even a subordinate to a Supreme Being, but a deceiving first angel. God in the classical meaning of the Creator does not exist. This doesn't stop Pullman equating his Authority with the God of the Jews and later of the Christians.

How might young people respond to this? One teenage Christian who had read *His Dark Materials* put it aptly: 'Pullman's god ain't my God and Pullman's church ain't my church.' Quite so. Yet many of Pullman's adolescent readers might be forgiven for being unable to draw the distinction, since no effort has been made to correct the identification of the true and living God whom Jesus honoured with the rather nasty God of *His Dark Materials*. It might almost have been calculated to leave the uninformed with the distinct feeling that God, however you look at him, is bad and his kingdom worse. Some will wish to raise the question as to whether schools should stock in their libraries or use as study materials books that denigrate the sincere religion of even a significant minority of their students.

God dies in *His Dark Materials*. Pullman explains: 'The God who dies is the God of the burners of heretics, the hangers of witches, the persecutors of Jews ... that God deserves to die.'[2] In the story it comes about like this. Serafina Pekkala manages to inveigle her way on board a ship where Mrs Coulter is torturing a witch to find out the truth of Lyra's identity and the prophecy concerning her life. Serafina, having put her sister witch out of her misery before she can betray the secret, goes on to discover from the consul of the witches that the Magisterium is assembling a great army. So she visits Lord Asriel's servant, Thorold, to discover his master's intentions, and finds that Asriel has gone into the other world, not to destroy the church, but to destroy the Authority himself; that is, the God of the church. Serafina questions whether this is possible and Thorold shares her doubts, since even angels couldn't do it.[3]

However, Asriel's ambition might just succeed where those angels had failed – especially if he comes into possession of the subtle knife, Aesahaettr, the God Destroyer, which Will is instructed to bring to him. Earlier the witch queen, Ruta Skadi, had paid Lord Asriel a visit and had sex with him, and he had invited the witches to join the army against the Authority. Asriel's army already numbered millions, but the Authority's was bigger, though

---

[2] Readerville Forum.

[3] This reflects John Milton's notion that there was a war in heaven before the creation of human beings. In Milton's scheme, the defeated angels were flung out of heaven and into hell for their pains.

its troops were old and either frightened or complacent. Discovering that Asriel needed the subtle knife, Ruta Skadi agreed to assist Will and Lyra.

Lyra became the prisoner of her own mother, but up in the mountains a local village girl named Ama had been bringing Mrs Coulter food, believing that she was a holy woman and that someone had put a trance on her daughter. Ama visits her local monastery to purchase a cure for Lyra and returning to the cave discovers the truth about Mrs Coulter. Meanwhile, everyone is searching for Lyra. The church wants her dead, of course. Will and Balthamos, and Iorek, and Lord Asriel, all want her alive. Asriel finds out what's going on with the aid of little spies called Gallivespians, aristocratic swordsmen riding dragonflies. They pretty well all arrive together, and Will confronts Mrs Coulter just as a battle is hotting up.

The knife gets broken because Will thinks about his mother. Nonetheless Will and Lyra and the two Gallivespians escape through a window, leaving Mrs Coulter unconscious, to be taken captive to Lord Asriel's fortress where he is preparing to join battle with the Metatron.

The showdown takes place as Will and Lyra emerge later from the abyss to lead out the dead. They come out right by Asriel's fortress, while the battle is raging. The ghosts engage in battle with the Spectres because just at that moment Will and Lyra simultaneously reach puberty and become prey to their ravenous power. At the same time Mrs Coulter takes the intention craft and flies to the clouded mountain, where she pretends to betray Lord Asriel and offers the Metatron the promise of sex. This lures the Metatron to the edge of the abyss where Lord Asriel is waiting, and he and Mrs Coulter heroically fight the Metatron, sacrificing their own lives to take him with them into the abyss and so save their daughter and the world.

As this is taking place, Will and Lyra come across a glass case in which lies the Ancient of Days. He is no less than a crumbling old ruin of an angel called God, but rather than killing him with the subtle knife they have compassion upon him, because he is so old and scared, crying like a baby and cowering in the corner of his crystal coffin. The subtle knife had been reforged by Iorek Byrnison and Will now uses it to cut through the crystal, so granting the demented and powerless old creature his freedom. He is as light as paper and completely in his dotage. A few moments later the wind catches him and he disintegrates. God, when they find him, is deserving only of pity and hardly worth the bother; he is too pathetic to waste your life on – a total irrelevancy.

John Milton shared something of Marcion's view of God, though from a more orthodox position. Certainly his understanding of God stressed the transcendence, power and majesty, not to say ruthlessness, of God. His was not a God in whose presence we would feel comfortable, and we might well long, as Marcion did, for a nicer divine being. This austere view of God was further reinforced by Milton's Arian[4] tendencies, which downplayed his understanding of God as revealed in the person of Jesus Christ. As a result, Milton portrayed a distorted God, which set the scene nicely for Pullman to turn him into some kind of devil.

The authoritarian character of Milton's heaven is just what we would expect if God were the usurper that Satan believes him to be. It leads to a ridiculous state of affairs in *Paradise Lost*, where God makes the good angels fight half their number for three days, knowing they will lose, and only wanting to prove to them that they are useless. The morale of the army must have been very low and it suggests a rather spiteful God playing a cruel game for his own amusement. Similarly, when Milton deals with Jesus, he contrasts the Father with his Son, as though the Son is a young knight errant, still callow and compassionate, being taught by a cynical battle-hardened Father who arrogantly toys with his enemies.

---

[4] Arianism: the view that Jesus was uniquely created and is a 'god', but not coequal with God the Father.

But it can't last; in the end Milton has God dissolve himself in some pantheistic manner into the matter of the universe. As with Philip Pullman in *His Dark Materials*, God abdicates with a sigh of relief. William Empson compared Milton's God to King Lear and Prospero,[5] both turbulent and masterful characters, but both struggling to enter peace. Maybe Milton looked on Oliver Cromwell like that too. After all, we can never separate Milton's work from his political involvement, and Cromwell seemed concerned to produce a good enough parliament so that he could allow himself to abdicate. So Milton will have Christ sacrifice himself to raise up the human race to such an extent that God is no longer needed because all the power has been given away and there is no need for a divine king.

This is a tenuous exegesis of Paul's words about Christ handing the kingdom back to God so that God may be all in all (1 Corinthians 15:27–28). It's highly improbable that Paul had in mind a precondition requiring the Father to dissolve himself into the material world. However, for Milton the material world was never independent of God, but was a part of God. So in a sense God simply returns to himself in *Paradise Lost*. But that is not a biblical concept.

Honest to God

God by definition defies definition. The clay doesn't master the potter nor the canvas the artist's vision. Creatures may know only what they are permitted to know – as God reminded Job, 'Canst thou by searching find out God?' (Job 11:7, AV). From a Christian perspective our knowledge of God comes by means of a threefold revelation. First, the in-your-face grandeur, beauty, intricacy, vastness, variety, awesomeness, vibrancy, cohesiveness and intelligence of God's book of works – the universe that declares his glory and demonstrates his craftsmanship. Second, his self-

---

5   William Empson, 'Heaven's Awful Monarch', *The Listener*, 21 July 1960.

revelation through the colourful lives and history of the characters whose stories and experiences constitute the books of the Bible. Then, thirdly, through God's greatest revelation of himself in Jesus Christ, the Son of God. As John the apostle and best friend of Jesus wrote, 'No-one has ever seen God, but God the One and Only, who is at the Father's side, has made him known' (John 1:18). Without a comprehensive and honest grasp of this threefold revelation we shall inevitably have a faulty view of God.

That honesty is hard to come by. We too easily seek to define God for our own convenience, personally or politically skewed to our vested interest and personal prejudices. It is no surprise that Milton should depict a God who is austere and chauvinistic, given his own character, let alone the political and intellectual climate of his day. Nor should we wonder that Pullman, in his desire for human autonomy over against all forms of authority, should cast God as a morally flawed, ageing and impotent relic, unworthy of our trust and allegiance.

Marcion's problem was that he viewed reality with one eye closed, and the good one at that, leaving him overwhelmed with despair. So he viewed God in the Old Testament only from the fire and brimstone perspective of Sinai, failing to recognise that Abraham was called the friend of God (James 2:23) or even to acknowledge the benevolent, inventive and almost playful God who made all things good and bestowed great blessings and joys on Adam and Eve. And he missed entirely the Mosaic message of God's love and his desire to bless his people, and David's wonderful intimacy with a God of mercy and compassion: 'As a father has compassion on his children, so the Lord has compassion on those who fear him; for he knows how we are formed, he remembers that we are dust' (Psalm 103:13–14). Perhaps Philip Pullman should note that God loves people formed of dust! And when we return to earthly dust, we want the words of Psalm 23, where the 'awful monarch' turns out to be the Lord my Shepherd.

This is not to take away from the tougher aspects of God's nature. Both Old and New Testaments do justice to God's obvious attributes of immortality, omniscience, omnipotence and omnipresence. God by his very nature is immortal, invisible and only wise, and no one has ever seen God at any time as he really is. Even in the New Testament he dwells in 'unapproachable light' (1 Timothy 6:15–16).

Rudolph Otto, in his book *The Idea of the Holy*, uses the term 'numinous' to describe this God-ness of God. He is transcendent, awesome, great and glorious. Yet he is also terrifyingly attractive and irresistible, like a great beauty, and our proper and unavoidable response to such an encounter with the living God is one of genuine worship and humility. This is good as far as it goes, but it leaves us with a scarcely knowable God, whereas the overriding message of the Bible is the desire and possibility of a genuine fellowship with him. In the words of an old hymn:

> Yet I may love Thee, too, O Lord,
> Almighty as Thou art,
> For Thou hast stooped to ask of me
> The love of my poor heart.

The Bible's message of reconciliation is all about this 'stooping' of God. When he created male and female in his own image, he immediately began the process of communication with his creation. If Adam and Eve hadn't sinned they could have learned with sheer fascination and delight all the mysteries of the universe and the secrets of God's heart. The Fall cut humans off from easy access to that knowledge, so revelation since then has come only through the painful process of hard learning in the vicissitudes of life – and with all the hindrances of corrupt and depraved human nature. So after the Fall began the lengthy process of education through history until the time was ripe for God to make himself known through the person of his Son, Jesus Christ. God most high became God most nigh – knowable, loveable, vulnerable, sacrificially laying down his life for us, inviting us into a personal relationship that culminates in the vision of the heavenly city where 'the dwelling of God is with men, and he will live with them. They will be his people, and God himself will be with them and be their God. He will wipe every tear from their eyes. There will be no more death or mourning or crying or pain, for the old order of things has passed away' (Revelation 21:3–4).

Given such a biblical view, we may well ask what goes wrong. Why do people find God so distant, impassive and in some cases, as with Pullman, tyrannical? Part of the problem may lie with the old Roman political paradigm, though it stretches back a lot further than the Roman Empire. Transfer the imperial pyramid with its top-down hierarchies of leadership into religion and God finishes up at the top of a hierarchy in the same way that Caesar was at the top of the Roman hierarchy. God's immanence is unavoidably sacrificed in favour of his transcendence, and he becomes effectively unknowable by ordinary mortals. Welcome then a specially trained and authorised priesthood to mete out access to God according to their dictates!

We might add to that the problems presented by the overthrow of Ptolemaic astronomy. The Greek astronomer, Ptolemy, had a humanist conception of the world that put the earth and man at the centre, with all the planets and the sun revolving around it. In spite of the appalling mathematics required to make it work, the idea held sway for several centuries until the Christians, Copernicus and Galileo, demonstrated that the sun was the centre of the solar system. Although this presented no serious problems for genuine lovers of God, others found themselves facing the most appalling alienation. They were suddenly lost in space and merely the third rock from the sun. God might be anywhere in such a vast universe. So the foundations were laid for the Enlightenment view of God that became known as Deism – the doctrine that God, having wound up the clockwork universe, went on holiday to a far distant corner, leaving us to manage as best we can. It was only a step from there to Unitarianism – the belief that God isn't a trinity, but a simple unity; a lonely, cold-blooded and absent Deity.

This is how John Milton seems to paint his picture of God; a cold, distant and somewhat poor second in personality to Satan.

Since Pullman reflects so much of Milton's view, it's hardly surprising that his vision of the Authority and his militant regent, the Metatron, is so bleak.

People can scarcely be blamed for finding God distasteful if he's presented in a manner so transcendent, unknowable and unsympathetic to our needs. We are left with little option but despair and cynicism or, as in the case of so much of the state religion in Britain and Europe, heroic stoicism. Faith comes across more as a survival course with a reward at the end if you're good enough, rather than a living experience of a loving God. The problem is made even worse when the state hijacks that kind of God for its own warlike ends, making him the instrument of oppression and violence rather than the merciful healer and deliverer. It's little wonder that many people rejected God in the trenches of the First World War. How could such a God, who apparently authorised and blessed the war, possibly draw near in love while they watched their comrades dying all around them in such appalling degradation? If it does nothing else, *His Dark Materials* challenges the church to revisit its classical theology and to sort itself out better on its doctrine of God.

The human spirit cries out for love and meaning. Given the prevailing Miltonian view of God, a reaction was inevitable, and it came in the form of Romanticism, championed by Rousseau in France and William Blake in England, among others. Romanticism represented a revolt against the repression of the human spirit and its desires for freedom. It was a revolution that the church should have been leading, not reacting against. The gospel should enshrine the heart-cry for love, passion, freedom and belonging. Instead it became a symbol of conservatism, maintaining the status quo of the privileged classes and imposing on all and sundry the virtues of severity. Little wonder people revolted – and that revolt was to continue into existentialism and the rise of rock culture. These might have been Christian movements, enshrining the gospel. Instead they turned out to be atheistic and pantheistic, because the church had allowed itself to be so identified with the cold formalism of Deism.

The people's republic

We may agree with Pullman that the God so often portrayed by the church deserves to die, but that God isn't really the God of the Bible, and Pullman's parody even less so. We are left with a choice: either we set out on the honest journey to discover 'the God and Father of our Lord Jesus Christ' or, apart from those who follow other religions altogether, we are left with trying to build the republic of heaven.

The problem with trying to destroy the kingdom of heaven and replace it with the republic of heaven is that it has been tried and it has never worked. The humanist republic inevitably leads to bondage, and if it's allowed to hijack the church, then it turns even the church into an instrument of bondage like itself. How many times have we heard politicians, philosophers and charlatans proclaim that they are going to set up a republic of heaven on earth, only to discover that it increases the sum of human misery? Rousseau's political thinking influenced the rise of the French Revolution, but how quickly that degenerated into a bloodbath. The same was true of the communist revolution. It was going to bring a new birth to the human race, 'a war in heaven' that would herald the coming of the new man. It did nothing of the sort; 200 million people and more lost their lives as a direct consequence of Communism, and countless more suffered repression, imprisonment, torture and deprivation.

Scientific atheism, social Darwinism, secular humanism, call them what they will, they never succeed for the simple reason that the hearts of the revolutionaries are in the same bondage as the hearts of those they perceive to be their tyrannical rulers. As Terry Pratchett put into the mouth of the incorruptible Vimes: 'Don't put your trust in revolutions. They always come round again. That's why they're called revolutions. People die, and nothing changes.'[6]

William Blake came to realise this for himself. Born in 1757, a self-educated Londoner, he was well read in the Bible, Milton and

---

[6] Terry Pratchett, *Night Watch* (Corgi, 2003), p.277.

Greek and Latin classical literature. He had a distinctly mystical view of the world and that seems to have been triggered by the death of his brother, Robert, when he saw his brother's soul 'ascend heavenwards clapping its hands for joy'. Blake became involved with London's psychics and, among others, with Emmanuel Swedenborg.

Blake took up the career of an engraver–poet–prophet and produced an extraordinary mixture of apocalyptic vision combined with political fervour. All of this was tangled up with a romanticist revision of Christian theology and with many psychological explorations. He also drew inspiration from the French Revolution and especially from the American Revolution of 1775 and the Declaration of Independence in 1873. He liked the idea of youthful, energetic rebels taking on the forces of autocratic authority.

In his work, Blake mythologised the American Revolution as an epic cosmic struggle between the forces of an authoritarian Jehovah known as Urizen and the figure of Orc, representing the young rebels. In essence he saw the conflict to be between the old regime of church and state and the radical libertarianism of youth. It is easy to see how this view has influenced Philip Pullman's plot in *His Dark Materials*. However, when the French Revolution gave way to the reign of terror, Blake became increasingly aware of the paradoxes and complexities of rebellion. It proved not to be as simple as he had first thought.

Pullman has a more romanticised and simplistic view. His revolution, led by the heroic crusader Lord Asriel and his amassed forces, succeeds well enough. The Metatron is destroyed, God is dead, the church has blown itself up and its allies are routed. With the Ancien Regime discarded, he is ready to build Blake's New Jerusalem in 'England's green and pleasant land', but with what? Will his warlike allies, some of them kings already, build the republic of heaven without tyranny? Violence begets violence. There is no way that Lord Asriel's republic of heaven could or would possibly have at its heart the serene values of the Mulefa.

Asriel is warlike and arrogant, so his republic would be the same. He wanted to pull down the Authority's fortress, but he had already built a fortress tower of his own from which he sought to govern. It could only replace one tyranny with another. It is the way of human republics to build towers, and always only the elite are allowed to inhabit them. The rest become cannon fodder.

If Asriel is bad, Mrs Coulter is no better. Quite apart from her unconvincing change of heart, she freely uses lies, deception and sexual seduction, all flavoured with the viciousness expressed by her monkey daemon. Why would any republic that included her be any better than the tyranny of the Authority? She would have made a spiteful ruler more akin to King Ahab's Jezebel than a woman of grace and peace. Any republic that included her would soon prove to be intolerant of all deviant opinions. In the event, of course, both she and Lord Asriel are killed off.

But would Will and Lyra do any better? A combination of his stoicism and her deceit would surely create a very cold and calculating government with little joy and little trust. For all the apparent heroism, there is nothing in *His Dark Materials* that holds out any hope of real happiness on earth – unless we wish to put our trust in the sum total of human consciousness. However, that requires us to believe, naively and unrealistically, in the inherent goodness of human nature – a notion that all human history and experience denies. Pullman seems to indicate that people are decent because people are decent; if so, he must inhabit a very precious and rarefied world, because it's certainly not true of the human race as a whole.

The political reality is different. Kill off heaven's awful monarch and we are more than likely to be left with earth's even worse tyrant.

9

Finding Grace

His Dark Materials is an extended metaphor for the journey from innocence to experience and is based upon an interpretation of Genesis 3 as suggested by Heinrich von Kleist. In other words, it is to do with growing up or coming of age, sexually and politically. Yet this attaining of full consciousness is ambivalent. There is a price to be paid, as Will and Lyra discover in their short-lived happiness. They, in the fashion of a classic Greek tragedy, make their heroic decision to sacrifice their newly found love for one another in order to save all the worlds, and then, like good humanists, must get on with the task of building the republic of heaven. Lyra herself will undergo an occult training in how to communicate with Dust, for this is the republic of heaven – spiritual politics – a co-operation between universal consciousness and mankind informing policy to bring about an age of bliss.

As we have seen, the first attempt at adulthood, i.e. the Garden of Eden, failed. The blame for this is put on God and the church, and both are charged with holding back human progress. Only by destroying their influence and taking another run at the Fall, and establishing the republic of heaven, can we hope to move forwards to a universal consciousness in which we will lose our self-consciousness and come of age.

What is true of the race as a whole is true of the individual. The implied formula seems very simple: rebel against your childhood faith in God, shake off the shackles of an authoritarian medieval church, embrace your emerging sexuality and discover sexual love. It may prove bittersweet, but you have become adult, and with stoical determination and a bit of mystical spirituality, you can take control of your own destiny and help build the republic of heaven.

Several observations might be made. First, however important growing up is, we must be careful not so to stress adulthood that we denigrate the value of childhood itself. An oft-voiced complaint about our current society is that children are expected to grow up too early and have less and less childhood to enjoy. The irony of this is that the full responsibilities of adulthood are pushed ever further into the future by both higher education and market forces.

Childhood is obviously very important in the Bible. Jesus said, 'Let the little children come to me, and do not hinder them, for the kingdom of God belongs to such as these' (Mark 10:14). It suggests there is something about childhood – perhaps an instinct for God, a fascination with life and a willingness to trust – that makes children by nature fitted for the kingdom of God. It has inspired the church globally to care for the well-being of children and to fight for their protection, health and education.

Yet just as Jesus 'grew in wisdom and stature, and in favour with God and men' (Luke 2:52) so must we. Contrary to the church in *His Dark Materials,* church leadership does not exist to keep people in subservient innocence; instead it seeks to equip the members of the church for their adult life and service to the community. Paul writes:

> ... so that the body of Christ may be built up until we all reach unity in the faith and in the knowledge of the Son of God and become mature, attaining to the whole measure of the fulness of Christ. Then we will no longer be infants, tossed back and forth by the waves, and

blown here and there by every wind of teaching and by the cunning and craftiness of men in their deceitful scheming. Instead, speaking the truth in love, we will in all things grow up into him who is the Head, that is, Christ. (Ephesians 4:12–15)

Good church leaders teach people how to discover the truth for themselves and how to apply it to their own lives.

Towards maturity

It is unnecessary to reject God or the church in order to attain maturity – unless we mean the God and church of Lyra's world, which were not worth having anyway. The Christian path is a process of maturation, both for individuals and for communities. People are meant to acquire an intelligent and practical understanding of the truth for themselves and to learn the adult discipline of distinguishing truth from falsehood. The writer to the Hebrews makes the point when he complains that his readers are wilfully failing to grow up: 'Solid food is for the mature, who by constant use have trained themselves to distinguish good from evil. Therefore let us leave the elementary teachings about Christ and go on to maturity' (Hebrews 5:14–6:1). This doesn't imply a growing away from Christ, but a growing up into Christ.

The apostle John uses the metaphor of growing up too. He attributes to children the simplicity of knowing that their sins have been forgiven and that they now have God as their heavenly Father. The young men, rather than being rebels, are in fact fighters for the truth. They have faced the challenges and taken on the evil one. In the process they have become strong and have learned for themselves the power and truth of the word of God, not because it's written on tablets of stone, but because it is written in their own heart experience of life. And he writes to the fathers as those who have reached a profound knowledge of God the Eternal One (1 John 2:12–14). It's not simply stuff gained by the intellect; it's the weather-beaten knowledge gained from trial and testing, through joys and sorrows, ups and downs, twists and turns, and that is the proper and legitimate goal for every true believer.

The apostle Paul had something similar in mind when he wrote his famous passage on love in 1 Corinthians 13. He says, 'When I was a child, I talked like a child, I thought like a child, I reasoned like a child. When I became a man, I put childish ways behind me' (1 Corinthians 13:11). So maturity for Paul was intimately wrapped up not with sexual maturation but with apprehending the love of God. That surely is what grace is all about. The merciful will of God is that those who rebelled in Eden should be restored not to a pristine innocence but to a life saturated with the love of God that enables them to grow without limit. It is worth labouring this point because the plot of *His Dark Materials* implies that the church, and indeed Christianity, is committed to keeping people in an infantile stage of obedience to its rules and regulations. It portrays a church that fights Dust in a misguided attempt at keeping people in innocence and is prepared to countenance the cruel severance of their souls to do so. In reality, nothing could be further from the truth.

His Dark Materials is more than simply a polemic against religion, however. Reflecting, as with Milton and Blake, a political milieu, it is a call to republicanism over against monarchism. From this perspective God and the church are representations of authoritarianism in all its forms. The violent overthrow of the heavenly king may be seen as a parable for the overthrow of earthly kings in favour of a democratic republic, and this may be viewed as a political system come of age. Or not. For we have already noted that revolutions notoriously fail to deliver the promised land. Growing up is a process, and by short circuiting the acquisition of wisdom, the new order is just as likely to be run by the foolish, with dire consequences for the rest of us.

Perhaps Pullman recognises this. His revolution is short lived and the real salvation of the human race proves not to be by the sword but by Will and Lyra's sexual fall. This salvation by the back door to Eden reverses the loss of consciousness brought about by the combined violence of the philosophers of Cittagazze, Lord Asriel's militarism and the church's fanatical attempt at destroying Lyra herself. It is to Will and Lyra and democracy that we must look for the future.

The jury will be out for a long time over whether democracy as we know it produces any kind of growing up, or even whether it actually offers any kind of real freedom. If a repressive religious system may keep society in immaturity, so might a pervasive liberalism with its own set of imposed values. In spite of apparent freedom, our society conforms to a remarkably limited system of beliefs. This creates problems for the idea of the republic of heaven. What will be its foundational values? Who will write its constitution or even its purpose? Surely not Lord Asriel? He has done his violence and died. Not Mary Malone. She has retreated into dreamland. We are left with Will and Lyra, and as we have seen they are actually ill-qualified for the task.

Maybe the future should be built with no values at all. Part of our problem with *His Dark Materials* is its own value system: its old-fashioned attack on the faith of others, its melodramatic heroics, its naive perspective on human goodness and its juvenile pantheism. The world has moved on and maybe in a postmodern environment no values will be needed for the future to evolve. Will this be the return to innocence where, much like the children in Lyra's world, our daemons will constantly change and we can believe everything and nothing with any certainty beyond our own experience? As is often attributed to G. K. Chesterton, 'When people cease to believe in God, they will believe in anything.'

Yet postmodern society, with its commitment to a plurality of values, is itself still controlled, and large numbers of people have no ability to think outside of the box simply because they are manipulated by the new priesthood of TV show-biz personalities, pundits and experts, and advertising executives. Even within the realms of science fresh thought is largely forbidden by a system that requires people to keep within the current theoretical paradigm if they want the grants and promotions. As Sir Arthur Eddington once said, and not necessarily with irony, 'One should never believe any experiment until it has been confirmed by theory.'

Liberation

The shorter roots of our postmodern society can be traced to the romantic existentialism of the 1960s, with its sexual liberation and abandonment of Christianity in favour of Eastern esoterism. 'All you need is love' sounds very good, but for all the justifiable rejection of wartime values in favour of freedom, it has hardly brought us paradise. This had nothing to do with slavery to a totalitarian church or political system, but with the fact that those philosophies and their outworking failed to address the real needs in society. So we are not convinced by Will and Lyra's efforts, and in their wistful memory of a happy moment we might see reflected no more than a youthful nostalgia for the short-lived sexual liberation of the 1960s and the general climate of freedom that surrounded it. The second 'happy sin', if that's what it be, offers no more than the first.

A lot depends on what we mean by growing up. It's all very well to reinterpret the Garden of Eden as a metaphor for the journey from innocence to experience and so make the Fall a good thing, but it fails totally to do justice to the reality of the evil that lurks in the human heart. Most humans with any degree of honesty are only too well aware of what they sometimes call the dark side of their nature. The purpose of Genesis 3 is to show us what we prefer to avoid – we have a problem of evil rather than of immaturity to contend with.

We have already seen that the Bible doesn't start with original sin but with original goodness. Adam and Eve were created in the image of God, in equality, harmony and unity with one another and their environment, and with their God. Since God declared their creation to be good, we may take it that their original innocence was not some childlike immature naivety, but a genuine goodness of heart. Nor were they children; Adam and Eve were created as sexually mature beings and, therefore, adult. They were capable of doing adult work and of raising children. God gave them instructions to do what he knew they were capable of doing.

So their state of innocence wasn't a state of ignorance so much as one of freedom from guilt and shame. There is no reason to suppose that Adam and Eve were not of great intellect and quite capable of the most profound understanding of the mysteries of life and the universe. If they had stayed faithful to God's will they would have produced a very different and very much better human race than the one we have today.

However, they were created free, and because their goodness wasn't some kind of platonic ideal, it was capable of corruption. Rebel they did, and sin and death entered the world with all its sorry consequences. God then became distant, not because he had ceased to love his creation, but because of the barrier erected by humans against his love and holiness. That offence against his nature and against the fundamental justice and morality of the universe by definition put us under condemnation. The God who made the laws of physics to hold the universe together cannot be arbitrary when it comes to the moral laws without being guilty of a self-contradiction, for that would make him no God and no good.

Yet God is love, and in the Garden of Eden – in a bit that Philip Pullman omitted – God promised that one day the seed of the woman, not Lyra but Jesus Christ, would in spite of being wounded himself crush Satan's authority (Genesis 3:15).

Jesus dealt with the heart of evil and its consequences, and he did so in the most poignant and passionate manner imaginable by offering himself as the ultimate sacrifice for the evils of human nature and society. In the classical words of the prophet Isaiah:

> Surely he took up our infirmities and carried our sorrows, yet we considered him stricken by God, smitten by him, and afflicted. But he was pierced for our transgressions, he was crushed for our iniquities; the punishment that brought us peace was upon him, and by his wounds

we are healed. We all, like sheep, have gone astray, each of us has turned to his own way; and the Lord has laid on him the iniquity of us all. (Isaiah 53:4–6)

Christ's sacrificial death on the cross was the means by which God reconciled the world to himself. Jesus became the epitome of sin, the scapegoat, the totally guilty one on behalf of the human race. He carried upon his own shoulders all the demands that justice could throw at the guilt of the human race. It was that act which removed all the barriers and fences between God and humankind and opened up the way for people to enter mutual fellowship with God. So Paul, commenting on the story of Adam and Eve, says:

Sin entered the world through one man, and death through sin, and in this way death came to all men, because all sinned ... so also the result of one act of righteousness was justification that brings life for all men. For just as through the disobedience of the one man many were made sinners, so also through the obedience of the one man the many will be made righteous. (Romans 5:12, 18–19)

Developing the thought, he adds in another place, 'For as in Adam all die, so in Christ all will be made alive' and later on he says, 'The first man Adam became a living being; the last Adam, a life-giving spirit' (1 Corinthians 15:22, 45).

The perverse intention of the serpent to effect a rift between God and man, and so provoke God to righteous anger and man to sullen rebellion, has been dealt with. Jesus has paid the representative price for the whole human race so that a new humanity can be birthed from the old, and that grants hope to everyone. People can be made right with God by faith because all that stood between them and God has been dealt with justly and fairly.

If Will and Lyra's stoical decision is noble and heroic, this is infinitely more so, and it truly changes hearts. As the prophet Ezekiel writes:

I will sprinkle clean water on you, and you will be clean; I will cleanse you from all your impurities and from all your idols. I will give you a new heart and put a new spirit in you; I will remove from you your heart of stone and give you a heart of flesh. And I will put my Spirit in you and move you to follow my decrees and be careful to keep my laws. (Ezekiel 36:25–27)

The answer to the world's needs is not a new Fall but a new covenant:

This is the covenant I will make with the house of Israel after that time, declares the Lord. I will put my laws in their minds and write them on their hearts. I will be their God, and they will be my people. No longer will a man teach his neighbour, or a man his brother, saying, 'Know the Lord,' because they will all know me, from the least of them to the greatest. For I will forgive their wickedness and will remember their sins no more. (Hebrews 8:10–12)

However naive or confusing it may seem, the genuine spiritual experience of uniting with Christ really does change people on the inside.

Yet to leave it there would open us justifiably to the charge of pietism. Inner liberation should lead to a transformation of society. It comes about through a revolution of love – what Richard Foster calls 'loving defiance' – against the injustices and corruption of the age. Revolutionaries will always argue that violence is the quickest way of getting things done, but that hardly benefits all the people who die and all those who are dispossessed because of the upheaval. Far better a revolution of love than one that involves guns and bombs. The future needs redemptive grace, not redemptive violence. Revolutionaries and governments alike, take note!

Significantly, Christ didn't come to earth with military might. That is what we should expect if salvation were simply a matter of liberation from the repressive power of political and religious systems. Similarly, the New Testament believers rejected violent political revolution. This was sensible in the given situation because it could only have led to an increase in oppression and suffering at the time, but it was also in accord with the spirit of Jesus. Nonetheless, the prophetic axe was laid to the root of the tree.

Slavery is a case in point. By all accounts it became common practice in the sub-apostolic age for people upon becoming Christians to release their slaves. Many of these were slaves because of debt, and the debt might extend as a labour commodity to their children as well as themselves. So it was an incredibly powerful expression of the jubilee principle that Jesus hinted at in his Nazareth manifesto.[1] Centuries later, Christians like Wilberforce argued persuasively and persistently for the abolition of slavery until at last they won their case. A hundred years earlier the Quakers had already abolished slavery on their own plantations. It may seem strange to our ears, but it was because black slaves were found capable of responding to the gospel that those who had treated them as less than human realised that they were, in fact, made in the image of God and so were entitled to full human rights. The non-Christians did not view them in such enlightened terms and continued to regard them as savages.

The civilising effect of the Christian faith continues to improve lives and communities. People testify not only to things such as getting their finances organised, clearing debts and reducing expensive vices such as smoking, gambling or alcohol intake, but to the profound hope and aspiration that is birthed within them. People who feel trapped in the system find themselves empowered by grace and they begin to take control of their destiny. This spills over into the shared life of the community and there is plenty of evidence of a reduction of crime, more stable families, more productive work and a release of creative endeavour as a direct consequence of the upraising grace of the gospel.

Christ's grace

What of the future? Pullman is right. We cannot return to paradise; we must go forwards to find grace. It seems that we can either

---

[1] 'The Spirit of the Lord is on me, because he has anointed me to preach good news to the poor. He has sent me to proclaim freedom for the prisoners and recovery of sight for the blind, to release the oppressed, to proclaim the year of the Lord's favour' (Luke 4:18–19).

choose the outmoded humanism of *His Dark Materials* and its attempt at building the republic of heaven by stoical self-determination and occult divination, or we can respond to the renewing grace of God in Jesus Christ. What is fairly certain is that people will not easily return to the old authoritarian expressions of Christianity. The years of what remains of the legalistic church are numbered and passing. People are rebelling against its strictures, not because they all want to live licentious and lascivious lives – though some do – but because they've seen however dimly that Jesus intended something better. As Mahatma Gandhi famously said in his day, 'If it weren't for Christians, I'd be a Christian.'

Rejecting the legalistic church doesn't have to lead to anarchy, atheism or even agnosticism. It can lead to a rediscovery of the logos, to Jesus Christ in all the Scriptures, in all creation and in all heaven. Indeed, the growing global church is largely made up of people who reject hierarchical legalism but who are also heartily sick of humanism and secularism. They're discovering Jesus afresh in such a way that their churches are entirely devoid of the characteristics of the church that Pullman parodies. The emerging new church is shot through with love and grace and isn't committed to a selfish agenda, but to the betterment of society as a whole. It really does exist for the benefit of its non-members, and it contains within its ranks minds of great brilliance and creativity, as well as many ordinary people. It offers the best hope for the future of society.

However, even at this point we must sound a note of caution. History would teach us, insofar as it teaches us anything, that those who attempt to bring the kingdom of God on earth inevitably fall into the very trap that Pullman sets. There is, after all, some justification for his attack on the medieval 'kingdom of God on earth' church. Just one example will suffice. Jan Huss of Bohemia (1369–1415) was a godly disciple of Wycliffe's writings and only wanted to see the church return to its New Testament roots – a laudable desire shared by many of us – yet the church persecuted

Huss and his followers, finally luring him into a trap by deceit and then burning him at the stake as a heretic. It opened a floodgate of troubles that were to lead in time to the Thirty Years War and to reduce Prague, from its role as a centre of learning and science, to a nonentity. People who do that sort of thing can by no stretch of credibility be called true disciples of Christ whatever their ecclesiastical pretensions, yet it's the kind of thing that happens when the church usurps its role and tries pre-emptively to establish the kingdom of God on earth.

The antidote to this is to recognise that the Christian hope extends beyond this life and beyond this age. However much grace and blessing may come from the gospel in the here and now, there is an expectation of a future and better age. It will not do to emphasise this at the expense of our responsibilities to those around us, but to deny it is to do despite to the resurrection of Christ and to his anticipated return. For one day the windows between the worlds will be opened, not with a subtle knife, but by the return of Jesus himself, in clouds and great glory. The worlds will meet and the cosmos as we know it will be changed. The heavens and the earth will pass away and all those who have died in Christ will be raised from the dead into some supraphysical state of perfect grace to enter the new heaven and the new earth that he has prepared for them. In contrast to *His Dark Materials*, which ends with the closing of all the windows, the return of Christ marks the opening of them – not to let Spectres loose, but to herald a whole new state of being. This upraising grace is available to all those who set their hope on the good King of kings and Lord of lords.

Pullman's work challenges the wrong sort of Christianity. In its place it offers us a vague pantheism coupled with a stoic determination. There is another alternative. It is to revisit the truly old religion – the faith that has its origin in a loving heavenly Father who created a world in which dwelt people made in his own image to love him and to be loved by him; the faith that in spite of the destructive effects of the Fall even in Eden foresaw the promise of a Redeemer that culminated in the coming of Jesus Christ; the faith that invites grace to do its upraising work in the heart and in society and that will one day allow us truly to grow up.

Jesus of Nazareth is the real hero of history and the real meaning of it all. It's his message to the human race, irrespective of culture or creed, that can enable those fallen sons of Adam truly to boast more blessings than their fathers lost. It beats dancing with the daisies, and it's certainly a lot better than bloody revolution or stoical survivalism.

The Christian gospel turns the world upside down because faith in the simple message of the crucified and risen Saviour breaks the shackles of demonic bondage, political oppression and personal alienation. God made his people to be free. That was his divine decree and desire. He made us to love and to be loved, and he wants us to grow into the fullness of his own Son. The conflict today isn't between divine autocracy and human will; it is between divine freedom and human bondage. The true kingdom of heaven – not Pullman's perverse parody – is a place of freedom. It always has been and always will be. Grace as so perfectly expressed in Jesus is an altogether better way of looking at the world. A man who committed no guile, no sin and no deceit, and who treated even his enemies with compassion, Jesus genuinely believed that love would triumph over violence, and he was right. We may at least hope that a kingdom modelled on his reign will make possible a new humanity.

A Closer Look at Harry Potter

by John Houghton

J K Rowling's *Harry Potter* series is uncontested as the greatest children's book phenomenon of all time.

Yet, while the world applauds, Christians are divided, and many are calling for the books to be banned from state schools and public libraries.

John Houghton himself is a writer of fantasy for children. In his book he offers an alternative to the secular wisdom on the conflict between good and evil. His considered critique offers timely and valuable insight for parents, teachers and all those involved in children's ministry.

This book is a must for all those who want to encourage a culturally literate, wise and godly generation who know how to have fun without regrets.

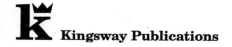
Kingsway Publications

A Closer Look at The Lord of the Rings

by Mark Eddy Smith

It has been voted the Best Book of the Century. It is one of the bestselling books ever. It is the basis for three major new motion pictures. It has inspired the whole genre of modern fantasy literature. It is a phenomenal epic crafted over many years by a scholar who has so far touched the hearts and aspirations of three generations.

That much is public knowledge. But less well known is the deeply Christian worldview of the author and the book. Mark Eddy Smith explores the values and themes which permeate the entire work and which bear fluent testimony to this overlooked but fundamental aspect to Tolkien's writing. And as we understand this Christian framework, we grasp so much more of the treasure Tolkien has bequeathed to the world.

Kingsway Publications